REFORM JUDAISM
A Jewish Way of Life

REFORM JUDAISM
A Jewish Way of Life

Rabbi Charles A. Kroloff

KTAV Publishing House, Inc.
Jersey City, New Jersey

Library of Congress Cataloging-in-Publication Data

Kroloff, Charles A.
  Reform Judaism: A Jewish Way of Life / Rabbi Charles A. Kroloff.
    p. cm.
  ISBN 0-88125-900-4
  1. Reform Judaism 1. Title
BM197.K76 2005
296.8'341–dc22

                                        2005018284

                        Published by

              KTAV Publishing House, Inc.
                    930 Newark Avenue
                  Jersey City, NJ 07306
                    orders@ktav.com
                      www.ktav.com
                  Tel (201) 963-9524
                  Fax (201) 963-0102

Typeset by Jerusalem Typesetting, www.jerusalemtype.com
Cover Design by Dororthy Wachtenheim

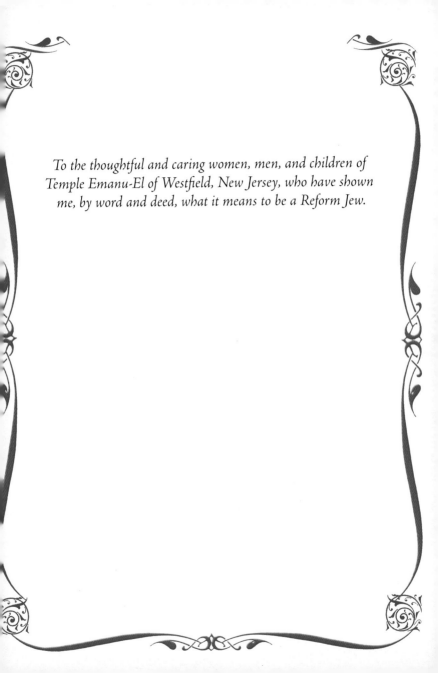

To the thoughtful and caring women, men, and children of Temple Emanu-El of Westfield, New Jersey, who have shown me, by word and deed, what it means to be a Reform Jew.

Acknowledgements

This book is intended to provide a taste of Reform Judaism for Jews and non-Jews alike. I hope that it will encourage the reader to explore the many facets of our liberal Jewish tradition through additional reading and practice. It also makes available, in handy form, basic prayers which a Jew may recite daily or weekly, in the synagogue, at home, or, as the v'ahavta prayer states, "on the way". Through Hebrew text, transliteration, and English translation, the blessings become accessible to all, irrespective of background or training.

My editor and friend, Adam Bengal, has a brilliant way of providing direction and critique. He knows how to propose reorganization of the text in a way that preserves the essence, but makes it much easier to study and digest. This is our third book together. Each collaboration has been for me a blessing. Bernard Scharfstein is a publisher with vision who has brought forth a wealth of Jewish publications that have sharpened our capacity to access our tradition and deepened our understanding of the human spirit. His contributions to Jewish learning have become legendary.

My appreciation goes forth to my colleagues who have read and commented on the manuscript, Rabbis Hillel Cohn,

Eric Gurvis, David Posner, Gerald Raiskin, Jeffrey Sirkman and Jonathan Stein. Their suggestions have enhanced the volume, while any shortcomings are, of course, mine.

Finally, and most significantly, I express my deep and abiding gratitude to my wife, Terry. For fifty exciting years, Terry has been my "in-house-editor", and best friend. Every time I write a page or deliver a talk, I can sense her insightful, practical, and caring counsel.

Rabbi Charles A. Kroloff
Westfield, New Jersey

Table of Contents

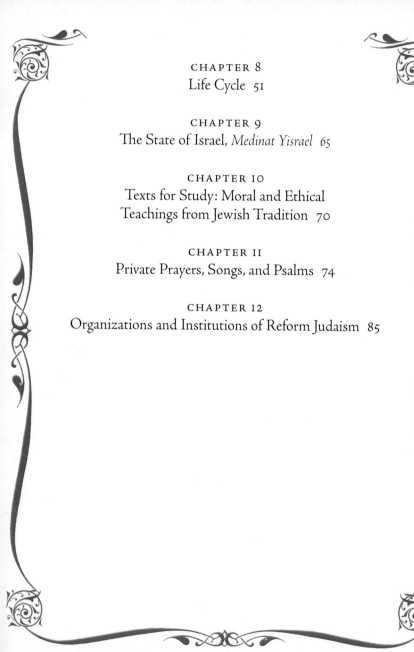

CHAPTER I

What Is Reform Judaism?

JUDAISM is one of the major religions of the world, with 13 million adherents worldwide. Six million reside in North America, five million in the State of Israel, and the remainder in many countries, especially France, Great Britain, and Russia. Judaism began nearly four thousand years ago, when Abraham, inspired by God, left his father's home and set out on a journey to the Promised Land of Canaan, which we know today as the Land of Israel. The Bible describes the amazing development of the Israelites, including the rich traditions and helpful laws that have guided individual Jews and the Jewish people to this day. Judaism is based on a strong belief in God, the holiness of Torah, and the mutual responsibility of Jews to one another and to all humanity.

The roots of Reform Judaism can be found in the history and literature of the Jewish people. From the Hebrew prophets, the Talmud, and rabbinic commentaries, we have learned that our traditions must be reinterpreted and trans-

formed to meet the new challenges of every era. Reform Judaism, the largest Jewish movement in North America, is rooted in tradition but committed to change.

The Reform Movement originated in Germany 200 years ago. Reform Judaism

- encourages us to study and respect Jewish teachings and traditions,
- expects us to use those teachings to deepen our lives ethically and morally, and to create a Jewish way of life.
- helps us to discover in our tradition profound sources of spiritual enrichment, enabling us to draw closer to God.
- calls on us to support the synagogue, the Jewish community, and the State of Israel, including equal rights for every Jew in Israel.

Reform Judaism applies Jewish values to solve problems in our society, championing the cause of civil rights, civil liberties, human rights, and anti-poverty programs. We call this process *tikkun olam*, repairing the world.

Committed to the absolute equality of women in all areas of Jewish life, Reform Judaism has opened its doors wide so that women can become rabbis, cantors, synagogue presidents, and serious students of Torah. In 1972, Sally Priesand became the first woman to be ordained in North America when she completed her rabbinical studies at Reform Judaism's Hebrew Union College. The movement has been the leader in outreach to interfaith families, in prayer book reform, and in bringing all Jews into full participation in synagogue life, regardless of sexual orientation.

With more than 900 synagogues and over a million members, united through the Union for Reform Judaism (URJ), the Reform Movement sponsors far-reaching programs for youth, a network of exceptional Jewish camps, Jewish education for all ages, the Religious Action Center in Washington, D.C., and publications that educate and inspire.

Hebrew Union College-Jewish Institute of Religion, with campuses in Cincinnati, Jerusalem, Los Angeles, and New York, ordains rabbis, invests cantors, and trains Jewish educators and community leaders for Reform Judaism and for the Jewish people in every corner of the globe. The Central Conference of American Rabbis publishes prayer books and other materials and supports the work of its members, 1,800 Reform rabbis worldwide. A full list of the institutions and organizations of Reform Judaism is found in Chapter 12.

CHAPTER 2

What Do Reform Jews Believe?

THERE is an old and healthy tradition of diversity in Judaism. Not all Jews think alike – not in the Bible, not in the Talmud, and certainly not in modern times. This independence of thought and belief is one of the hallmarks of present-day Reform Judaism. Reform Jews are encouraged to ask probing questions about God, prayer, Torah, and all of the fundamental ideas of Judaism. Torah, the foundation of Jewish Life, is discussed in Chapter 3.

God

Reform Jews believe in God. But not all of us believe exactly the same about God. Many of us believe in a "personal God" who cares about us, who hears prayer, who is with us and sustains us in times of suffering or crisis. For others, God is more transcendent, a great power or force that operates as a moral spirit in the universe. Some of us feel that God can be described as the "still, small voice" of conscience within

us. Fundamental to Judaism is the idea that God is One and that we human beings are partners with God in making the world a better place. Some Reform Jews describe themselves as agnostics or even atheists. They too are part of the family of Reform Judaism.

Spirituality is an important theme in Jewish life. A contemporary Jewish thinker, Arthur Green, helps us understand this idea:

> Spirituality is a view of religion that sees its primary task as cultivating and nourishing the human soul or spirit. Each person, according to this view, has an inner life that he or she may choose to develop; this "inwardness" goes deeper than the usual object of psychological investigation and cannot fairly be explained in Freudian or other psychological terms. Ultimately, it is "transpersonal," reaching beyond the individual and linking him/her to all other selves and to the single Spirit or Self of the universe we call God. God is experientially accessible through the cultivation of this inner life.
>
> *Restoring the Aleph: Judaism for the Contemporary Seeker*

Prayer

Prayer also means different things to different Reform Jews. Some of us feel that we have experienced God's response to our prayers: prayers for health, for reconciliation, for accept-

ing difficult circumstances, for peace. Others view prayer as a way to transcend our finite being and to connect with a power or spirit beyond ourselves. And there are some who feel that prayer consists primarily of a spiritual conversation with oneself.

Abraham Joshua Heschel was one of the greatest Jewish thinkers and social activists of the twentieth century. Here is what he has said about prayer:

> Prayer serves many aims. It serves to save the inward life from oblivion. It serves to alleviate anguish. It serves to partake of God's mysterious grace and guidance. Yet, ultimately, prayer must not be experienced as an act for the sake of something else. We pray in order to pray. ... To pray is to open a door, where both God and soul may enter.
>
> *Understanding Jewish Prayer*, Jakob Petuchowski, Ktav, pp. 71–72.

Rabbi Heschel also wrote:

> Prayer invites God to let God's presence suffuse our spirits, to let God's will prevail in our lives.
>
> Prayer cannot bring water to parched fields, nor mend a broken bridge, nor rebuild a ruined city.
>
> But prayer can water an arid soul, mend a broken heart, and rebuild a weakened will. (adapted)

The Hebrew word for prayer is *tefilah*. Its Hebrew root, in the reflexive form, means "to examine oneself." Prayer helps us to look within, to see ourselves as God might see us.

Tikkun Olam, Mending the World

Reform Jews believe that social justice is central to being a Jew. We believe that every act of goodness we perform furthers God's purpose on earth.

The mystical tradition of Kabbalah teaches us that, when the world was created, countless "sparks of the divine" were scattered throughout the world. Jews are expected to help bring those sparks together into one great light of justice and goodness. This mending the world is called *tikkun olam.* Reform Judaism's Religious Action Center in Washington, D.C., helps us focus on this goal.

We can "mend the world" in so many ways:

+ distributing food to the hungry
+ visiting the sick
+ mentoring an inner-city student
+ registering citizens to vote
+ add your ideas to this list

Tzedakah, performing righteous deeds, is a personal form of social justice. Athough *tzedakah* is often translated as "charity," its literal meaning is "righteousness." One of the ways that we live a righteous life is by performing good deeds, including contributing to worthy causes

It is customary to offer *tzedakah* in honor of a newborn child, a bar or bat mitzvah, a confirmation, graduation, mar-

riage, or a significant accomplishment. Contributions are also appropriate in memory of someone who has recently died or on the occasion of a *yahrzeit* (the anniversary of a death).

Maimonides, the great twelfth-century Jewish philosopher, known also as the Rambam, taught that there are eight levels of *tzedakah*, beginning with the lowest:

1. To give grudgingly, reluctantly, or with regret
2. To give less than one should, but with grace
3. To give what one should, but only after being asked
4. To give before one is asked
5. To give without knowing who will receive it, although the recipient knows the identity of the giver
6. To give without making known one's identity
7. To give so that neither giver nor receiver knows the identity of the other
8. To help another to become self-supporting, by means of a gift or a loan or by finding employment for the one in need

We believe that human beings are created in the image of God and that every life is precious. According to tradition, "If a person saves one life it is as though that person saved the whole world." Jews are taught that saving a life takes precedence over all other responsibilities. We are expected to forgo ritual obligations, including Shabbat observance

and fasting on Yom Kippur, in order to preserve life. Reform Jews also encourage organ donation for the purpose of saving or healing a life.

Tikkun HaNefesh, Mending the Soul

Reform Jews believe that we must also focus on our inner life. There are many ways to approach the inner life. They include prayer, meditation, study, and song. Although some of us find fulfillment by engaging in such activities alone, being with a community of Jews who share our goals can enhance the experience. The synagogue offers many ways to move in this direction. *Chavurot* or *kallot* are small groups that gather in synagogues or at retreats for personal Jewish growth.

Shalom

Reform Jews believe in the pursuit of peace, or *shalom*. The prophet Isaiah taught:

> "And they shall beat their swords into plowshares and their spears into pruning hooks. Nation shall not lift sword against nation, neither shall they learn war anymore."

Judaism is dedicated to putting an end to conflict between nations and peoples. But *shalom* means more than the absence of war. According to the Talmud, "The whole of the Torah is for promoting peace." *Shalom* comes from the Hebrew root letters, *ShLM,* meaning "whole" or "complete."

It refers to harmonious relations between human beings and between nations, and to respect for all of God's creation, including the environment.

One of the most beautiful prayers in Jewish tradition is

עֹשֶׂה שָׁלוֹם בִּמְרוֹמָיו, הוּא יַעֲשֶׂה שָׁלוֹם עָלֵינוּ, וְעַל כָּל יִשְׂרָאֵל, וְעַל כָּל בְּנֵי אָדָם, וְאִמְרוּ אָמֵן.

Oseh shalom bimromav, hu ya'aseh shalom aleinu v'al kol Yisrael, v'al kol b'nei adam, v'imru amen.

May God, who makes peace in the high places, bring peace to us, to all Israel, and to all humanity, and let us say, amen.

The Synagogue

Reform Jews believe that the synagogue is the central institution of the Jewish people. According to tradition, the synagogue has three primary functions: *bet tefilah*, *bet midrash*, and *bet k'nesset*, a house of prayer, a house of study, and a house of assembly.

Reform synagogues offer Jewish education for children and adults, early childhood programs, religious services, holiday celebrations, social justice activities, community outreach, rabbinic counseling, Jewish music, and groups for youth, adult singles, the newly or partly retired, and seniors. Synagogues support Israel and offer caring community programs which assist the recently bereaved, the sick, and the homebound.

All Jews should belong to a synagogue and all Jew-

ish children should receive a Jewish education. If financial considerations present an obstacle to membership, all synagogues are prepared to make special arrangements. Synagogue staff may include one or more rabbis, cantor, educators, executive director, youth leaders, program director, and early childhood director. Some synagogues may have as few as twenty families, while others may be as large as one or two thousand family units. Whether large, small, or medium size, the synagogue, together with the home, is the place "where Jews are made."

Outreach

Reform Judaism is more interested in building bridges than in erecting barriers. We care very much about inclusion and very little about exclusion. We welcome expressions of interest in Judaism, whether for the purpose of study or the possibility of conversion. Outreach to interfaith families, a hallmark of Reform Judaism since 1979, has encouraged tens of thousands of intermarried persons to experience religious renewal in our synagogues and to become a part of the Jewish future.

Our synagogues and the Union for Reform Judaism (URJ) offer classes which introduce non-Jews and unaffiliated Jews to the wondrous tradition of the Jewish people. A short course, "Taste of Judaism", and a longer one, "Introduction to Judaism", available in most communities, open new doors for those in search of Jewish meaning and connection. Feel free to contact the local rabbi or the regional office of the URJ for information on registration.

Interfaith couples are warmly welcome in Reform synagogues. They participate actively in nearly all aspects of synagogue life and their children experience full acceptance within the congregation. While we hope that the non-Jewish partner will convert before marriage or after, we encourage them, in any event, to learn about Judaism and to find spiritual fulfillment within our faith. The establishment of a Jewish home and a Jewish way of life invariably brings enrichment to the family and strength to the Jewish people.

Jews do not actively proselytize. We dispatch no missionaries encouraging non-Jews to convert. However, if someone who is not Jewish expresses an interest in learning about Judaism and the possibility of conversion, he or she will find Reform rabbis and the synagogue as a whole receptive and ready to help. The process of converting involves establishing a relationship with the rabbi and/or cantor, engaging in a serious program of Jewish learning, participating in the life of the synagogue and the Jewish community, and making a personal commitment to become part of the Jewish people. The duration of time for such a process will vary, but may range from less than a year to several years, depending on the requirements of the rabbi and the intensity of the process.

CHAPTER 3

What Is Torah?

*R*EFORM Jews, like most other Jews, believe that Torah is the foundation of our faith. In the broadest terms, Torah is the totality of Jewish tradition, law, history, and ethics. It refers to the entire body of Jewish learning which has been and continues to be the basis for Jewish life and faith. Torah literally means "instruction."

Torah refers most specifically to the parchment scroll which occupies the central position in the *Aron HaKodesh*, the Holy Ark in the synagogue. Written by hand by a *sofer* or scribe, the Torah scroll consists of the first five books of the Bible – Genesis, Exodus, Leviticus, Numbers, and Deuteronomy – known also as the *Chumash*.

In its Principles for Reform Judaism (1999), the Central Conference of American Rabbis stated: "We cherish the truths revealed in Torah, God's ongoing revelation to our people and the record of our people's ongoing relationship with God."

Most synagogues have available in the pews or on a

shelf a Torah commentary, which consists of the Hebrew text, English translation, and extensive commentaries, ancient and modern. These books, like most Jewish prayer books, open from right to left, which is the way Hebrew is written. These commentaries, filled with insight, can be studied on your own or with a rabbi or teacher, often before the Shabbat morning service, or at adult learning courses offered in every synagogue.

Other important books of Jewish tradition, such as the Mishnah and the Talmud, are based on the five books of Torah. Chapter 4 explains how readings from the Torah are used in the synagogue every Shabbat.

When we study Torah or engage in any form of Jewish learning, we say:

בָּרוּךְ אַתָּה יְיָ אֱלֹהֵינוּ מֶלֶךְ הָעוֹלָם, אֲשֶׁר קִדְּשָׁנוּ בְּמִצְוֹתָיו, וְצִוָּנוּ לַעֲסוֹק בְּדִבְרֵי תוֹרָה.

Baruch ata Adonai, Eloheinu melech ha'olam, asher kid'shanu b'mitzvotav v'tzivanu la'asok b'divrei Torah.

Blessed are You, Adonai, our God, Sovereign of the universe, who makes our lives holy through mitzvot and commands us to study words of Torah.

(*Mitzvah* means "commandment." *Mitzvot* is the plural of *mitzvah*.)

CHAPTER 4

The Service in a Reform Synagogue

*J*EWISH prayer in the synagogue is usually led by a rabbi and cantor, although any knowledgeable Jew, not necessarily clergy, is permitted to officiate. Music plays a central role in Jewish prayer. The cantor, who leads the musical portions, will draw not only upon traditional melodies, but also contemporary ones, some of which have become popular among Jewish youth.

Jews pray in the morning (the service is known as *shacharit*); in the afternoon (*mincha*), and in the evening (*maariv*). The afternoon and evening services are often united as one.

Jewish prayer has a clear structure. Briefly, it looks something like this on Shabbat:

Praise and thanksgiving, with songs and psalms
Call to worship which introduces
Sh'ma and its blessings
Amidah

Torah reading
Sermon or *d'var Torah* (Torah lesson)
Concluding prayers

Many Jewish men and some Jewish women wear a *tallit* or prayer shawl on Shabbat morning and at certain other times of prayer. It is worn in fulfillment of commandments that appear in the Torah. A *kippah*, also known as a *yarmulke*, is worn as head covering by most, but not all, male Jews and by some female Jews during a religious service. The following prayer is said when one is putting on the *tallit*.

בָּרוּךְ אַתָּה יְיָ אֱלֹהֵינוּ מֶלֶךְ הָעוֹלָם, אֲשֶׁר קִדְּשָׁנוּ בְּמִצְוֹתָיו, וְצִוָּנוּ לְהִתְעַטֵּף בַּצִּיצִת.

Baruch ata Adonai Eloheinu melech ha'olam asher kid'shanu b'mitzvotav v'tzivanu l'hitateif batzitzit.

Blessed are You, Adonai our God, Sovereign of the universe, who makes our lives holy through mitzvot and commands us to wrap ourselves in the tallit.

The morning service for Shabbat commences with *P'sukei d'zimrah*, verses of praise, mostly from Psalms. As Lawrence Hoffman, a prominent Reform rabbi and Professor of Liturgy at Hebrew Union College, has observed, these offerings may be seen as "prayer before prayer. They function as the warm-up for the morning service, recognition that prayerfulness cannot be summoned on demand."

The service continues with the *Sh'ma* and its Blessings, which begins with the *Bar'chu*, the call to worship. In the call to worship, the leader, in effect, asks whether the congrega-

tion is ready to bless God and the worshippers respond by singing a strong praise of God.

The *Sh'ma* is the Jew's central declaration of faith. It affirms the unity of God as expressed by the Jewish people since Biblical times.

שְׁמַע יִשְׂרָאֵל, יְיָ אֱלֹהֵינוּ, יְיָ אֶחָד.

Sh'ma Yisrael Adonai Eloheinu, Adonai Echad

Listen, O Israel, Adonai is our God, Adonai is One!

The *Sh'ma* includes a paragraph beginning "V'ahavta...," You shall love *Adonai* your God with all your heart, with all your soul, and with all your being.

A declaration following the *Sh'ma*, *Mee chamocha*, celebrates the Exodus from Egypt, the parting of the Red Sea, and the power of God.

Amidah, or "the standing prayer" is the primary prayer of the Jewish service. Also known as *t'filah* or "the prayer," it begins with praise and ends with thanksgiving.

A silent prayer following the *Amidah* is a precious opportunity for personal meditation.

On Shabbat (as well as on Mondays and Thursdays) we read from the Torah (the Five Books of Moses). Each week a portion (*parashah*) from Torah is assigned to be read so that, by the end of the year at the holiday known as Simchat Torah (joy of Torah), the entire scroll has been heard. It is inspiring to consider that in nearly every synagogue throughout the world the same portion is read, thus strengthening our spiritual bonds with Jews in every land.

The honor of blessing the Torah is known as an *aliyah*. Other honors include lifting the scroll (*hagbah*) and redressing the scroll (*g'lilah*).

The following blessing is said before the reading of the Torah portion:

בָּרְכוּ אֶת יְיָ הַמְבֹרָךְ.

בָּרוּךְ יְיָ הַמְבֹרָךְ לְעוֹלָם וָעֶד.

בָּרוּךְ אַתָּה יְיָ אֱלֹהֵינוּ מֶלֶךְ הָעוֹלָם, אֲשֶׁר בָּחַר בָּנוּ מִכָּל הָעַמִּים וְנָתַן לָנוּ אֶת תּוֹרָתוֹ. בָּרוּךְ אַתָּה יְיָ, נוֹתֵן הַתּוֹרָה.

Bar'chu et Adonai ham'vorach

(Cong: Baruch Adonai ham'vorach l'olam va'ed)

Baruch Adonai ham'vorach l'olam va'ed

Baruch ata Adonai Eloheinu melech ha'olam, asher bachar banu mikol ha'amim, v'natan lanu et torato. Baruch ata Adonai, notein hatorah.

Praise Adonai who deserves to be praised.

(Cong: Praised be Adonai, who deserves to be praised forever and ever.)

Praised be Adonai, who deserves to be praised forever and ever.

Blessed are You, Adonai our God, Sovereign of the universe, who has chosen us from all peoples and given us Your Torah. Blessed are You, Adonai, Giver of the Torah.

After the reading, the following blessing is said:

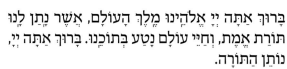

בָּרוּךְ אַתָּה יְיָ אֱלֹהֵינוּ מֶלֶךְ הָעוֹלָם, אֲשֶׁר נָתַן לָנוּ
תּוֹרַת אֱמֶת, וְחַיֵּי עוֹלָם נָטַע בְּתוֹכֵנוּ. בָּרוּךְ אַתָּה יְיָ,
נוֹתֵן הַתּוֹרָה.

*Baruch ata Adonai Eloheinu melech ha'olam, asher natan
lanu torat emet v'chayei olam nata b'tocheinu. Baruch ata
Adonai, notein hatorah.*

Blessed are You, Adonai our God, Sovereign of the
universe, who has given us a Torah of truth and has
implanted within us eternal life. Blessed are You,
Adonai, Giver of the Torah.

Following the Torah service, the rabbi will usually deliver a sermon which is also known as a *d'var Torah*. Often
related to the Torah portion of the week, the rabbi's sermon
may discuss issues dealing with personal ethics, national or
international concerns, Israel, theology, prayer, values, family, our Jewish way of life, the Jewish people, interfaith, and
much more.

The service continues with the *Aleinu* prayer which
acknowledges the power and universality of God and our
unique history of searching for the Eternal. We conclude
by naming those who have died recently and at this time
in years past (*yahrzeit*). The Mourner's *Kaddish* expresses
our trust in God, even at a time of personal loss. (See
Chapter 8)

CHAPTER 5

Bar and Bat Mitzvah and Jewish Education

*J*EWISH education begins in the Jewish home. In the earliest years, the Jewish child learns at home from songs, blessings, candles, pictures, and ritual objects, all of which create a positive Jewish atmosphere from the day the baby arrives home. When parents celebrate Jewish life in the home and then in the synagogue, they set a beautiful example for their children.

Preschool sponsored by the synagogue or a Jewish Community Center reinforces that experience. On Shabbat and at holiday times, synagogues offer "Tiny Tot" programs which are available also to nonmembers. When children are ready for school, as early as kindergarten, they should be enrolled in the synagogue's program of religious education and/or in a Jewish day school, especially if a liberal one is available.

Remember: it is never too early to bring Jewish life to a child. It is appropriate to recite the *shehecheyanu* blessing (see Chapter 8) when a child begins a new phase of Jewish learning.

Bar and Bat Mitzvah

According to Jewish tradition, a boy reaches his religious maturity on his thirteenth birthday, and a girl reaches hers at twelve. Since Reform Judaism treats boys and girls equally, we designate thirteen as the time when every Jewish youngster is expected to fulfill the commandments and is no longer viewed as a minor in Jewish life. This means, for example, that a boy or girl of thirteen may be counted in a *minyan* (ten persons required for most religious services). Bar Mitzvah means, literally, "son of the commandment." Bat Mitzvah means "daughter of the commandment."

The idea that a boy or girl is subject to the law at a specific age goes back nearly 2,000 years to the days of the Talmud, but having a special ceremony in which a boy of thirteen is called up to read from the Torah is only about five centuries old. The first Bat Mitzvah in the United States was Judith Kaplan Eisenstein, who was called to the Torah in 1922 at the New York City synagogue led by her father, Rabbi Mordecai Kaplan, the founder of the branch of Judaism known as Reconstructionism. The first recorded Bat Mitzvah at a Reform synagogue took place in 1931.

Although a Bar or Bat Mitzvah ceremony is not required for a Jewish boy or girl to be considered an "adult," most Jewish children do participate in such a ceremony, which can be a wondrous religious experience. It is usually held on Shabbat morning; the youngster is called to chant from Torah and chant the Haftarah (a section from the Prophets, which has a theme related to the Torah portion read that day), leads part of the service, and offers a *d'var Torah* (an explanation and interpretation of the Torah portion). Synagogues require a minimum number of years of study of Jewish history, traditions, and Hebrew before such a ceremony may take place. That study, as well as "mitzvah projects" or good works in the community, are what endow the Bar or Bat Mitzvah ceremony with its central meaning.

Bar or Bat Mitzvah should definitely not be an end to the child's Jewish education. On the contrary, it should be seen as an opportunity for the students to use the abilities they have acquired to lead the congregation in prayer and learning and then to commit themselves to continued Jewish study through Confirmation and beyond, and to a Jewish way of life.

Bar and Bat Mitzvah provide a time for family and friends to gather in celebration of Jewish growth and learning. Social festivities should be modest in scale, in keeping with Jewish values, never ostentatious, and should be accompanied by *tzedakah* contributions to worthy causes.

Confirmation

In grades eight through ten, Jewish learning is elevated to a new and more mature level, a chance to discuss with the rabbi, cantor, and others such subjects as God, ethical dilemmas, interfaith issues, Jewish life at college, sex, love, and marriage. In contrast to Bar and Bat Mitzvah, which is primarily an individual experience, Confirmation offers students the opportunity to bond as a class and to build enduring Jewish relationships. Many Confirmation classes participate in retreat weekends and travel as a group to Israel or other Jewish communities in the United States or abroad.

In most Reform synagogues, the ceremony of Confirmation occurs after the tenth grade (sometimes eleventh or twelfth) on or near the festival of Shavuot in May or June. Confirmation was an innovation of Reform Judaism in the nineteenth century to celebrate at least ten years of Jewish education. The first Confirmation service in the Western hemisphere was held in the Virgin Islands in 1844.

Most synagogues offer post-Confirmation programs through high school graduation.

College

College can mean an interruption in students' connection with the synagogue and the Jewish community. But it does not have to be that way! Many rabbis encourage their students to consider only colleges and universities that have a significant Jewish presence on campus. That could mean a Jewish student body of 15 to 20 percent or more, a Hillel program, or a local Jewish community that takes a strong, proactive interest in Jewish students on campus. Go to www.hillel.org and view Hillel's database at "Guide to Jewish Life on Campus."

Many synagogues send "Jewish care packages" to their college students at Chanukah, Purim, Pesach, and other holidays, as well as the monthly temple bulletin. Some rab-

bis make annual visits to campuses that have a number of students from their synagogue. A College Student Shabbat and socials at vacation time help students maintain their Jewish connections. College years are a challenging time for Jewish life, but with ingenuity and follow-through, bonds can be forged and maintained.

Lifetime Jewish Education

Jewish tradition teaches us, "A Jew should never stop studying until the day of death." In other words, for a Jew, study and personal spiritual growth should be viewed as a lifetime opportunity. Most synagogues offer adult study programs with the rabbi, cantor, and other faculty. These include Torah study, Talmud, Midrash, Jewish history, American Jewish community, life cycle, holidays, and Hebrew language. Some programs lead to a Bar or Bat Mitzvah ceremony for adults or to an adult Confirmation. All lead to the sense of fulfillment which comes from spiritual and intellectual growth.

CHAPTER 6
Shabbat

S HABBAT is the most important day in the Jewish year. Since it comes every week, you might think that it would be less important than a holiday that occurs just once a year. But, no, precisely because it occurs weekly, Shabbat sets the tone for every day in the life of the Jew. Ahad HaAm, an eminent Zionist writer, taught, with much truth: "Even more than Israel has kept the Shabbat, the Shabbat has kept Israel."

Shabbat is the Hebrew word for "Sabbath." Shabbat begins at sunset on Friday and ends with sunset on Saturday. Shabbat may be welcomed on Friday evening with an early Kabbalat Shabbat service in the synagogue. Many Reform and Conservative synagogues hold a later service (starting between 7:30 and 8:30 PM). Those services include the blessing over wine (*Kiddush*) and, in Reform temples, the lighting of Shabbat candles. Jewish families gather at home – after the early service or before the late service – to welcome Shabbat with candles, Kiddush wine, and challah (twisted egg bread), songs (see Chapter 11), and blessings for children and grandchildren. A feeling of great warmth and love surrounds the Shabbat table. Jews also come to synagogue for Shabbat observance on Saturday morning, and sometimes later that day.

Abraham Joshua Heschel describes Shabbat in his beautiful book *The Sabbath*:

> Time is like a wasteland. It has grandeur, but no beauty. Its strange, frightful power is always feared, but never cheered. Then we arrive at the seventh day, and the Shabbat is endowed with a felicity which enraptures the soul, which glides into our thoughts with a healing sympathy. It is a day on which hours do not oust one another. It is a day that can soothe all sadness away.
>
> (*The Sabbath*, Farrar Straus and Giroux, p. 20)

Shabbat Blessings

Here are some of the beautiful blessings you might read or sing on Friday evening:

BLESSING THE CANDLES:

As we kindle these lights, we begin a holy time. May we and all Israel find in it renewal of body and spirit, and the sense that You are near to us at all times. (*On the Doorposts*, Central Conference of American Rabbis, p. 38)

בָּרוּךְ אַתָּה יְיָ אֱלֹהֵינוּ מֶלֶךְ הָעוֹלָם, אֲשֶׁר קִדְּשָׁנוּ בְּמִצְוֹתָיו, וְצִוָּנוּ לְהַדְלִיק נֵר שֶׁל שַׁבָּת.

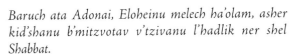

Baruch ata Adonai, Eloheinu melech ha'olam, asher kid'shanu b'mitzvotav v'tzivanu l'hadlik ner shel Shabbat.

Blessed are You, Adonai our God, Sovereign of the universe, who makes our lives holy through mitzvot and commands us to kindle the lights of Shabbat.

KIDDUSH FOR SHABBAT:

בָּרוּךְ אַתָּה יְיָ אֱלֹהֵינוּ מֶלֶךְ הָעוֹלָם, בּוֹרֵא פְּרִי הַגָּפֶן.

בָּרוּךְ אַתָּה יְיָ אֱלֹהֵינוּ מֶלֶךְ הָעוֹלָם, אֲשֶׁר קִדְּשָׁנוּ בְּמִצְוֹתָיו וְרָצָה בָנוּ, וְשַׁבַּת קָדְשׁוֹ בְּאַהֲבָה וּבְרָצוֹן הִנְחִילָנוּ זִכָּרוֹן לְמַעֲשֵׂה בְרֵאשִׁית, כִּי הוּא יוֹם תְּחִלָּה לְמִקְרָאֵי קֹדֶשׁ, זֵכֶר לִיצִיאַת מִצְרָיִם, כִּי בָנוּ בָחַרְתָּ וְאוֹתָנוּ קִדַּשְׁתָּ מִכָּל הָעַמִּים, וְשַׁבַּת קָדְשְׁךָ בְּאַהֲבָה וּבְרָצוֹן הִנְחַלְתָּנוּ. בָּרוּךְ אַתָּה יְיָ, מְקַדֵּשׁ הַשַּׁבָּת.

Baruch ata Adonai, Eloheinu melech ha'olam, borei p'ri hagafen.

Baruch ata Adonai, Eloheinu melech ha'olam, asher kid'shanu b'mitzvotav v'ratza vanu, v'shabbat kodsho, b'ahava uv'ratzon hinchilanu, zikaron l'ma'asei v'reisheet. Ki hu yom t'chila l'mikra'ei kodesh, zeicher litziat Mitzrayim. Ki vanu vacharta v'otanu kidashta mikol ha'amim, v'shabbat kodsh'cha b'ahava uv'ratzon hinchaltanu. Baruch ata Adonai, m'kadesh hashabbat.

Blessed are You, Adonai our God, Sovereign of the universe, Creator of the fruit of the vine.

Blessed are You, Adonai our God, Sovereign of the universe, who makes our lives holy through the mitzvah

of Shabbat: the sign of Your love, a reminder of Your creative work, and of our liberation from Egyptian bondage, our day of days. On Shabbat especially, we hear Your call to serve You as a holy people. Blessed are You, Adonai, for the holiness of Shabbat.

(Adapted from *On the Doorposts*, p. 42)

PARENTS' BLESSING OF CHILDREN:

Family blessing

We thank You, God, for our family and for what we mean and bring to each other. Help us to be modest in our demands of one another, but generous in our giving to each other. May we never measure how much love or encouragement we offer; may we never count the times we forgive. Rather, may we always be grateful that we have one another and that we are able to express our love in acts of kindness. Keep us gentle in our speech. When we offer words of criticism, may they be chosen with care and spoken softly. May we waste no opportunity to speak words of sympathy, appreciation, and praise. Bless our family with health, happiness, and contentment. Above all, grant us the wisdom to build a joyous and peaceful home in which Your spirit will always abide. (From *Likrat Shabbat*, Sidney Greenberg.)

For a boy

יְשִׂמְךָ אֱלֹהִים כְּאֶפְרַיִם וְכִמְנַשֶּׁה:

Y'simcha Elohim k'Efrayim uchiM'nasheh.

May God inspire you as Ephraim and Menasheh,

who carried forward the faith and traditions of our people.

For a girl

יְשִׂמֵךְ אֱלֹהִים כְּשָׂרָה רִבְקָה רָחֵל וְלֵאָה:

Y'simeich Elohim k'Sarah, Rivkah, Rachel v'Leia

May God inspire you as Sarah, Rebecca, Rachel, and Leah, who carried forward the faith and traditions of our people.

For all children

יְבָרֶכְךָ יְהֹוָה וְיִשְׁמְרֶךָ:
יָאֵר יְהֹוָה פָּנָיו אֵלֶיךָ וִיחֻנֶּךָ:
יִשָּׂא יְהֹוָה פָּנָיו אֵלֶיךָ וְיָשֵׂם לְךָ שָׁלוֹם:

Y'va-rech'cha Adonai v'yishm'rehcha.
Ya'eir Adonai panav eilecha vichu-neka.
Yisa Adonai panav eilecha v'yaseim l'cha shalom.

May Adonai bless you and take care of you.
May the spirit of Adonai shine upon you in all that you do.
May Adonai lift up the Divine spirit upon you and give you peace.

BLESSING BEFORE EATING:

בָּרוּךְ אַתָּה יְיָ, אֱלֹהֵינוּ מֶלֶךְ הָעוֹלָם, הַמּוֹצִיא לֶחֶם מִן הָאָרֶץ.

Baruch ata Adonai, Eloheinu melech ha'olam, hamotzi lechem min ha'aretz.

Blessed are You, Adonai our God, Sovereign of the

universe, who causes bread to come forth from the earth.

Birkat HaMazon, Blessing after Meals

Most of us have been taught from childhood not to take the food we consume for granted and to appreciate how others have labored long and hard to bring nourishment to our table. We have learned that we must respect and take good care of our planet, which is a precious gift from God. One of the ways that we demonstrate our gratitude and our love for God is by preserving and protecting God's creation.

Birkat HaMazon is the traditional prayer which Jews chant after the Shabbat meal. Some Jews recite this blessing after every meal to give thanks to God for the food we eat. When you chant the *Birkat,* it will draw you closer to those seated around the table, to all the Jewish people, and to God.

FOR SHABBAT AND YOM TOV:

שִׁיר הַמַּעֲלוֹת, בְּשׁוּב יְיָ אֶת שִׁיבַת צִיּוֹן, הָיִינוּ
כְּחֹלְמִים. אָז יִמָּלֵא שְׂחוֹק פִּינוּ וּלְשׁוֹנֵנוּ רִנָּה, אָז
יֹאמְרוּ בַגּוֹיִם, הִגְדִּיל יְיָ לַעֲשׂוֹת עִם אֵלֶּה. הִגְדִּיל יְיָ
לַעֲשׂוֹת עִמָּנוּ, הָיִינוּ שְׂמֵחִים. שׁוּבָה יְיָ אֶת שְׁבִיתֵנוּ,
כַּאֲפִיקִים בַּנֶּגֶב. הַזֹּרְעִים בְּדִמְעָה, בְּרִנָּה יִקְצֹרוּ. הָלוֹךְ
יֵלֵךְ וּבָכֹה נֹשֵׂא מֶשֶׁךְ הַזָּרַע, בֹּא יָבֹא בְרִנָּה נֹשֵׂא
אֲלֻמֹתָיו.

*Shir hama'alot b'shuv Adonai et shivat tziyon hayinu
k'chol'mim. Az yimalei s'chok pinu, ul'shoneinu rina. Az
yomru vagoyim, higdil Adonai la'asot im eileh. Higdil*

Adonai la'asot imanu, hayinu s'meichim. Shuva Adonai et sh'viteinu ka'afikim banegev. Hazorim b'dima b'rina yiktzoru. Haloch yeileich uvacho, nosei meshech hazara, bo yavo b'rina nosei alumotav.

When God restored the exiles to Zion, it seemed like a dream. Our mouths were filled with laughter, our tongues with joyful song. Then they said among the nations: God has done great things for them. Yes, God is doing great things for us, and we are joyful. Restore our fortunes, O God, as streams revive the desert. Then those who have sown tears shall reap in joy. Those who go forth weeping, carrying bags of seeds, shall come home with shouts of joy, bearing their sheaves.

(*Psalms,* Jewish Publication Society)

For all occasions:

LEADER

חֲבֵרֵי נְבָרֵךְ!

Chaveirei n'vareich

Let us praise God.

GROUP

יְהִי שֵׁם יְיָ מְבֹרָךְ מֵעַתָּה וְעַד עוֹלָם.

Y'hi shem Adonai m'vorach mei'ata v'ad olam.

Praised be the name of Adonai, now and always.

LEADER

יְהִי שֵׁם יְיָ מְבֹרָךְ מֵעַתָּה וְעַד עוֹלָם. בִּרְשׁוּת חֲבֵרַי,
נְבָרֵךְ (אֱלֹהֵינוּ) שֶׁאָכַלְנוּ מִשֶּׁלּוֹ.

Y'hi shem Adonai m'vorach mei'ata v'ad olam. Birshut chav'rei n'varech (Eloheinu) she-achalnu mishelo.

Praised be the name of Adonai, now and always.

GROUP

בָּרוּךְ (אֱלֹהֵינוּ) שֶׁאָכַלְנוּ מִשֶּׁלּוֹ וּבְטוּבוֹ חָיִינוּ.

Baruch (Eloheinu) she-achalnu mishelo uv'tuvo chayinu.

Praised be our God who has provided food for us to eat.

LEADER

בָּרוּךְ (אֱלֹהֵינוּ) שֶׁאָכַלְנוּ מִשֶּׁלּוֹ וּבְטוּבוֹ חָיִינוּ.

Baruch (Eloheinu) she-achalnu mishelo uv'tuvo chayinu.

Praised be our God who has provided food for us to eat and by whose goodness we live. Praised be God and praised be God's name.

GROUP

בָּרוּךְ הוּא וּבָרוּךְ שְׁמוֹ.

בָּרוּךְ אַתָּה יְיָ, אֱלֹהֵינוּ מֶלֶךְ הָעוֹלָם, הַזָּן אֶת הָעוֹלָם כֻּלּוֹ בְּטוּבוֹ בְּחֵן בְּחֶסֶד וּבְרַחֲמִים, הוּא נוֹתֵן לֶחֶם לְכָל בָּשָׂר כִּי לְעוֹלָם חַסְדּוֹ. וּבְטוּבוֹ הַגָּדוֹל תָּמִיד לֹא חָסַר לָנוּ, וְאַל יֶחְסַר לָנוּ מָזוֹן לְעוֹלָם וָעֶד. בַּעֲבוּר שְׁמוֹ הַגָּדוֹל, כִּי הוּא אֵל זָן וּמְפַרְנֵס לַכֹּל וּמֵטִיב לַכֹּל, וּמֵכִין מָזוֹן לְכָל בְּרִיּוֹתָיו אֲשֶׁר בָּרָא. בָּרוּךְ אַתָּה יְיָ, הַזָּן אֶת הַכֹּל.

Baruch hu uvaruch sh'mo.

Baruch ata Adonai, Eloheinu melech ha'olam, hazan et ha'olam kulo b'tuvo, b'chein, b'chesed, uv'rachamim.

Hu notein lechem l'chol basar, ki l'olam chasdo. Uv'tuvo hagadol tamid lo chaser lanu v'al yechsar lanu mazon l'olam va'ed, ba'avur sh'mo hagadol, ki hu Eil zan um'farnes lakol, umeitiv lakol umeichin mason l'chol b'riyotav asher bara. Baruch ata Adonai, hazan et hakol.

Praised are You, Adonai, our God, Sovereign of the universe, who sustains the entire world with goodness, kindness, and mercy. God provides nourishment to all flesh, for God's kindness is eternal. Through God's great goodness, we do not lack sustenance. Praised are You, Adonai, the Source of sustenance for all.

כַּכָּתוּב, וְאָכַלְתָּ וְשָׂבָעְתָּ, וּבֵרַכְתָּ אֶת יְיָ אֱלֹהֶיךָ עַל הָאָרֶץ הַטֹּבָה אֲשֶׁר נָתַן לָךְ. בָּרוּךְ אַתָּה יְיָ, עַל הָאָרֶץ וְעַל הַמָּזוֹן.

Kakatuv v'achalta v'savata uvei-rachta et Adonai Elohecha, al ha'aretz hatova asher natan lach. Baruch ata Adonai, al haaretz v'al hamazon.

As it is written: "You shall eat and be satisfied and praise Adonai, your God, for the good land God has given to us. Praised are You, Adonai, for the earth and for sustenance.

וּבְנֵה יְרוּשָׁלַיִם עִיר הַקֹּדֶשׁ בִּמְהֵרָה בְיָמֵינוּ. בָּרוּךְ אַתָּה יְיָ, בּוֹנֵה בְרַחֲמָיו יְרוּשָׁלָיִם. אָמֵן.

Uv'nei Yerushalayim ir hakodesh bimheira v'yameinu. Baruch ata Adonai, bone v'rachamav Yerushalayim, amen.

And may Jerusalem, the holy city, be renewed speedily in our time. Praised are You, Adonai, who renews Jerusalem in compassion.

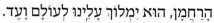

הָרַחֲמָן, הוּא יִמְלוֹךְ עָלֵינוּ לְעוֹלָם וָעֶד.

Harachaman, hu yimloch aleinu l'olam va'ed.

May the Merciful One rule over us forever.

הָרַחֲמָן, הוּא יִשְׁלַח לָנוּ בְּרָכָה מְרֻבָּה בַּבַּיִת הַזֶּה, וְעַל
שֻׁלְחָן זֶה שֶׁאָכַלְנוּ עָלָיו.

Harachaman, hu yishlach lanu b'racha m'ruba babayit hazeh, v'al shulchan zeh she-achalnu alav.

May the Merciful One send us abundant blessing in this dwelling and upon this table where we have eaten.

הָרַחֲמָן, הוּא יְבָרֵךְ אֶת מְדִינַת יִשְׂרָאֵל.

Harachaman, hu y'varech et medinat Yisrael.

May the Merciful One bless the State of Israel.

ON SHABBAT:

הָרַחֲמָן, הוּא יַנְחִילֵנוּ יוֹם שֶׁכֻּלּוֹ שַׁבָּת וּמְנוּחָה לְחַיֵּי
הָעוֹלָמִים.

Harachaman, hu yanchileinu yom shekulo Shabbat, um'nucha l'chayei ha'olamim.

May the Merciful One help us to experience a time that is entirely Shabbat, a time of everlasting peace.

ON YOM TOV:

הָרַחֲמָן, הוּא יַנְחִילֵנוּ יוֹם שֶׁכֻּלּוֹ טוֹב.

Harachaman, hu yanchileinu yom shekulo tov.

May the Merciful One help us to experience a time that is all goodness.

Shabbat

FOR ALL OCCASIONS:

עֹשֶׂה שָׁלוֹם בִּמְרוֹמָיו, הוּא יַעֲשֶׂה שָׁלוֹם עָלֵינוּ וְעַל כָּל יִשְׂרָאֵל, וְאִמְרוּ אָמֵן.

Oseh shalom bimromav, hu ya'aseh shalom aleinu v'al kol Yisrael, v'imru, amen.

May God, who makes peace in the high places, bring peace to us and to all Israel, and let us say, Amen.

יְיָ עֹז לְעַמּוֹ יִתֵּן, יְיָ יְבָרֵךְ אֶת עַמּוֹ בַשָּׁלוֹם.

Adonai oz l'amo yitein, Adonai y'vareich et amo vashalom.

May God give strength unto God's people. May God bless Israel and all humanity with peace.

Kiddush for Shabbat Morning

וְשָׁמְרוּ בְנֵי־יִשְׂרָאֵל אֶת־הַשַּׁבָּת לַעֲשׂוֹת אֶת־הַשַּׁבָּת לְדֹרֹתָם בְּרִית עוֹלָם: בֵּינִי וּבֵין בְּנֵי יִשְׂרָאֵל אוֹת הִוא לְעֹלָם כִּי־שֵׁשֶׁת יָמִים עָשָׂה יְיָ אֶת־הַשָּׁמַיִם וְאֶת־הָאָרֶץ וּבַיּוֹם הַשְּׁבִיעִי שָׁבַת וַיִּנָּפַשׁ:

עַל־כֵּן בֵּרַךְ יְיָ אֶת־יוֹם הַשַּׁבָּת וַיְקַדְּשֵׁהוּ:

בָּרוּךְ אַתָּה יְיָ אֱלֹהֵינוּ מֶלֶךְ הָעוֹלָם, בּוֹרֵא פְּרִי הַגָּפֶן.

V'shamru v'nei Yisrael et hashabbat, la'asot et hashabbat l'dorotam b'rit olam. Beini uvein b'nei Yisrael ot hi l'olam, ki sheishet yamim asah Adonai et hashamayim v'et ha'aretz, uvayom hash'vi'i shavat vayinafash.

Al kein beirach Adonai et yom hashabat vay'kadd'sheihu.

Baruch ata Adonai, Eloheinu melech ha'olam, borei p'ri hagafen.

The people of Israel shall keep the Shabbat, to observe the Shabbat in all generations as a covenant forever. It is a sign forever between Me and between the people of Israel, for in six days Adonai made heaven and earth, and on the seventh day God ceased and was refreshed.

Therefore Adonai blessed the seventh day and made it holy.

Blessed are You, Adonai our God, Sovereign of the universe, Creator of the fruit of the vine.

Havdalah

As the sun sets on Saturday afternoon, Jews mark the end of Shabbat with a brief but moving ritual known as *Havdalah*. This tradition separates our Shabbat day of rest, prayer, study, and recreation from the rest of the work week.

Havdalah means "separation." Through this ceremony of prayer, song, and symbol, we relish, for just a little longer, the joy of Shabbat; we reluctantly give up the delight of Shabbat and prepare for the obligations and opportunities of the new week, knowing that – in just six days – Shabbat will return. When celebrating *Havdalah* in a family or synagogue group, we often join hands as we strengthen our bonds with each other and with our tradition.

The leader raises the cup of wine or grape juice.

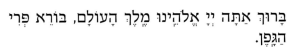

בָּרוּךְ אַתָּה יְיָ אֱלֹהֵינוּ מֶלֶךְ הָעוֹלָם, בּוֹרֵא פְּרִי הַגָּפֶן.

Baruch ata Adonai, Eloheinu melech ha'olam, borei p'ri hagafen.

Blessed are You, Adonai our God, Sovereign of the universe, who creates the fruit of the vine.

The leader lifts the spice box.

בָּרוּךְ אַתָּה יְיָ, אֱלֹהֵינוּ מֶלֶךְ הָעוֹלָם, בּוֹרֵא מִינֵי בְשָׂמִים.

Baruch ata Adonai, Eloheinu melech ha'olam, borei minei v'samim.

Blessed are You, Adonai our God, Sovereign of the universe, who creates many kinds of spices.

Pass around the spice box and let all inhale its fragrance.

The leader holds up the *Havdalah* candle.

בָּרוּךְ אַתָּה יְיָ, אֱלֹהֵינוּ מֶלֶךְ הָעוֹלָם, בּוֹרֵא מְאוֹרֵי הָאֵשׁ.

Baruch ata Adonai, Eloheinu melech ha'olam, borei m'orei ha'eish.

Blessed are You, Adonai our God, Sovereign of the universe, who creates the light of fire.

We have been taught to distinguish between sacred and secular, between holy and mundane. The distinction is real, but not final: the commonplace can be sanctified. That is our task in the week ahead: to find holiness in the everyday

experiences of life. As we conclude Shabbat, we remind ourselves that the time of redemption has not yet arrived. But with the best efforts of women and men of goodwill, redemption will come.

(Adapted from *Siddur Lev Chadash*, Union of Liberal and Progressive Synagogues, London, 1995)

בָּרוּךְ אַתָּה יְיָ, אֱלֹהֵינוּ מֶלֶךְ הָעוֹלָם, הַמַּבְדִּיל בֵּין קֹדֶשׁ לְחוֹל, בֵּין אוֹר לְחֹשֶׁךְ, בֵּין יִשְׂרָאֵל לָעַמִּים, בֵּין יוֹם הַשְּׁבִיעִי לְשֵׁשֶׁת יְמֵי הַמַּעֲשֶׂה: בָּרוּךְ אַתָּה יְיָ, הַמַּבְדִּיל בֵּין קֹדֶשׁ לְחוֹל:

Baruch ata Adonai, Eloheinu melech ha'olam, hamavdil bein kodesh l'chol, bein or l'choshech, bein Yisrael l'amim, bein yom hash'vi-i l'sheishet y'mei hama'aseh. Baruch ata Adonai, hamavdil bein kodesh l'chol.

Blessed are You, Adonai our God, Sovereign of the universe, who distinguishes between the holy and the mundane, between light and darkness, between Israel and the nations, between the seventh day and the six days of work. Blessed are You, Adonai, who distinguishes between the holy and the mundane.

The candle is extinguished in the cup of wine.

We sing together *Eliyahu HaNavi*, Elijah the Prophet:

אֵלִיָּהוּ הַנָּבִיא, אֵלִיָּהוּ הַתִּשְׁבִּי, אֵלִיָּהוּ, אֵלִיָּהוּ, אֵלִיָּהוּ הַגִּלְעָדִי, בִּמְהֵרָה בְיָמֵנוּ, יָבוֹא אֵלֵינוּ עִם מָשִׁיחַ בֶּן דָּוִד, עִם מָשִׁיחַ בֶּן דָּוִד, אֵלִיָּהוּ הַנָּבִיא...

Eiliyahu hanavi, Eiliyahu hatishbi, Eiliyahu, Eliyahu, Eiliyahu hagiladi, Bimheirah v'yameinu, yavo eileinu, Im

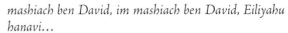

Shabbat

mashiach ben David, im mashiach ben David, Eiliyahu hanavi…

Elijah the prophet, Elijah the Tishbite, Elijah, Elijah, Elijah the Giladite, Come soon to us, with the Messiah, son of David.

(Although the song refers to the Messiah, Reform Jews believe in the coming of a Messianic age, or time of redemption.)

שָׁבוּעַ טוֹב, שָׁבוּעַ טוֹב, שָׁבוּעַ טוֹב, שָׁבוּעַ טוֹב!

Shavua tov, shavua tov, shavua tov, shavua tov!

A good week, a week of peace; may gladness reign and joy increase.

CHAPTER 7

The Jewish Year

T HE Jewish calendar is based on the lunar rather than the solar calendar. Therefore, the dates of Jewish holidays in the secular calendar will vary from year to year, but will always occur in the same season.

Rosh Hashanah and Yom Kippur

The holiest period of the Jewish year falls sometime during September and early October. It begins with Rosh Hashanah, which initiates a ten-day period of spiritual self-reflection, culminating in Yom Kippur, the Day of Atonement. In between those High Holy Days are the ten days of repentance which are especially holy – a time for taking a "spiritual inventory" (*cheshbon hanefesh*) of ourselves.

Rosh Hashanah, which literally means the beginning of the year, is also known as the "Day of Judgment" and the "Day of Remembrance," highlighting the central themes of the day. One of the most powerful moments of the Rosh

Hashanah service is the sounding of the *shofar* or ram's horn. Its purpose is to wake us from our spiritual and moral lethargy and to call us to repentance. The prayer book used on these holy days is known as the *Machzor*. Some Reform synagogues observe only one day of Rosh Hashanah (in keeping with the Biblical prescription and as observed in Israel). Many Reform congregations celebrate two days, as do all Conservative, Orthodox, and Reconstructionist synagogues.

Yom Kippur is the most solemn day of the Jewish year. Jews fast from sunset to sunset in keeping with the Biblical commandment: "On the tenth day of the seventh month is the Day of Atonement …and you shall practice self-denial. It shall be to you a Shabbat of solemn rest." (Leviticus 23:27, 32.) On the eve of Yom Kippur, the *Kol Nidre* prayer, with its plaintive, emotional chant, fills us with awe and heightens our sense of repentance. The *Yizkor* memorial service during the day recalls those who have died during the previous twelve months and in years past. Jews are expected to remain in the synagogue all day, until the holy day concludes with the brief but powerful service known as *Ne'ilah*. The fast concludes with one great blast of the *shofar*.

The following candle blessing is said for *Yom Tov*, that is, for holy days and festivals:

בָּרוּךְ אַתָּה יְיָ אֱלֹהֵינוּ מֶלֶךְ הָעוֹלָם, אֲשֶׁר קִדְּשָׁנוּ בְּמִצְוֹתָיו וְצִוָּנוּ לְהַדְלִיק נֵר שֶׁל (שַׁבָּת וְשֶׁל) יוֹם טוֹב.

Baruch ata Adonai, Eloheinu melech ha'olam, asher kid'shanu b'mitzvotav v'tzivanu l'hadlik ner shel (Shabbat v'shel) Yom Tov.

Blessed are You, Adonai our God, Sovereign of the universe, who makes our lives holy through mitzvot and commands us to kindle the lights of (Shabbat and) Yom Tov.

Sukkot

Five days after Yom Kippur we celebrate the Festival of Sukkot (*Chag HaSukkot*), known also as the Feast of Tabernacles or Booths. A *sukkah* is a small, temporary dwelling which reminds us of the huts the Israelites used in the Sinai wilderness when they fled from slavery in Egypt. Jews today build a *sukkah* in their backyards, on their roof tops, and alongside their synagogues, and eat as many meals as possible in the *sukkah* during the festival.

Our ancestors could never have survived their life in flimsy tents in the desert were it not for their faith in God. Sukkot celebrates that historic journey to freedom and to the Promised Land. It is a time of abundant thanksgiving for the fruits of nature and for God's protection.

Sukkot lasts for seven days for most Reform Jews (eight for Conservative and Orthodox). On entering a *sukkah*, we say:

בָּרוּךְ אַתָּה יְיָ אֱלֹהֵינוּ מֶלֶךְ הָעוֹלָם, אֲשֶׁר קִדְּשָׁנוּ בְּמִצְוֹתָיו וְצִוָּנוּ לֵישֵׁב בַּסֻּכָּה.

Baruch ata Adonai, Eloheinu melech ha'olam, asher kid'shanu b'mitzvotav v'tzivanu leisheiv basukkah.

Blessed are You, Adonai our God, Sovereign of the universe, who makes our lives holy through mitzvot and commands us to dwell in the *sukkah.*

In the *sukkah*, as well as at services during Sukkot, we wave the *lulav*, or palm branch, in all directions and say:

בָּרוּךְ אַתָּה יְיָ אֱלֹהֵינוּ מֶלֶךְ הָעוֹלָם, אֲשֶׁר קִדְּשָׁנוּ
בְּמִצְוֹתָיו, וְצִוָּנוּ עַל נְטִילַת לוּלָב.

Baruch ata Adonai, Eloheinu melech ha'olam, asher kid'shanu b'mitzvotav v'tzivanu al n'tilat lulav.

Blessed are You, Adonai our God, Sovereign of the universe, who makes our lives holy through mitzvot, and commands us to wave the *lulav.*

On the first night, we also say the *Shehecheyanu* blessing. (See Chapter 8.)

Simchat Torah

Simchat Torah follows immediately upon the conclusion of Sukkot. Literally, "the joy of the Torah," this is a particularly joyous and uplifting holiday, a time when we finish reading the last verses of Deuteronomy, the final book of Torah, and, without taking a breath, begin again to read the opening verses of Genesis. Simchat Torah is marked by dancing with the Torah scrolls, flags for the children, holiday refreshments, fun, and games. Not to be missed!

In Israel and in many Reform synagogues, Simchat Torah is combined with Shemini Atzeret, which is a festival in its own right that celebrates the conclusion of Sukkot.

Eight Nights of Chanukah

Chanukah symbolizes the victory of the few over the many and the triumph of freedom and faith over degradation and paganism. It inspires us all to stand up for our principles and not give up our traditions or beliefs in favor of fads or cheap culture just because they may be popular.

In 165 BCE, the Hasmonean family, led by Judah Maccabee, drove the Syrians out of the land of Israel and rededicated the Temple in Jerusalem, which had been defiled by the enemy. The Talmud records that the Maccabees found only a single cruse of oil for the Eternal Light, enough to last one day. But miraculously, the oil lasted for eight days. We therefore celebrate Chanukah by lighting the Chanukah menorah, known as the *Chanukiyah*, for eight days. The Haftarah (prophetic reading) for Chanukah is taken from the prophet Zechariah: "Not by might, nor by power, but by My spirit, says Adonai."

Candles are placed in the *Chanukiyah* from right to left and are lit from left to right. An extra candle known as the *shamash* is used to light one candle on the first night, two on the second, and onward until we conclude with eight lights on the eighth night.

When we light the *Chanukiah*, we say the following blessings:

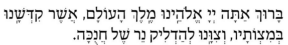

בָּרוּךְ אַתָּה יְיָ אֱלֹהֵינוּ מֶלֶךְ הָעוֹלָם, אֲשֶׁר קִדְּשָׁנוּ בְּמִצְוֹתָיו, וְצִוָּנוּ לְהַדְלִיק נֵר שֶׁל חֲנֻכָּה.

Baruch ata Adonai, Eloheinu melech ha'olam, asher kid'shanu b'mitzvotav v'tzivanu l'hadlik neir shel Chanukah.

Blessed are You, Adonai our God, Sovereign of the universe, who makes our lives holy through mitzvot and commands us to kindle the lights of Chanukah.

בָּרוּךְ אַתָּה יְיָ אֱלֹהֵינוּ מֶלֶךְ הָעוֹלָם, שֶׁעָשָׂה נִסִּים לַאֲבוֹתֵינוּ בַּיָּמִים הָהֵם בַּזְּמַן הַזֶּה.

Baruch ata Adonai, Eloheinu melech ha'olam, she-asah nisim la-avoteinu bayamim haheim baz'man hazeh.

Blessed are You, Adonai our God, Sovereign of the universe, who performed wonders for our ancestors in ancient times, at this season.

On first night only, we also say the *Shehecheyanu* prayer. (See Chapter 8.)

In North America, Jews are accustomed to giving gifts on Chanukah. Gifts should be given in moderation, in keeping with the spirit of the holiday, and should include *tzedakah* (see Chapter 1). In Israel, gift-giving is associated more with the holiday of Purim than with Chanukah.

Purim

Purim may be one of the so-called minor festivals of Judaism, but it certainly has a powerful attraction to Jews of all ages. It is based on the Biblical Book of Esther, which relates that

Haman and his henchmen plotted the destruction of the Jews of Persia. They were saved by the courage of Queen Esther and her cousin, Mordecai, who foiled Haman's evil intentions. By celebrating the victory of the Jewish people over tyrants, we are demonstrating how important it is to display personal courage and to identify strongly with fellow Jews.

On Purim, we gather to read from the *Megillah*, which is the Scroll of Esther. Some remarkable customs are associated with Purim. They include dressing in costume (anything from Mordecai to Mickey Mouse), graggers (noisemakers), merrymaking, eating *hamantaschen* (a three-cornered pastry filled with fruit or poppy seeds) and *sh'lach manot*, gift-giving, not only to family and friends, but to persons in need. Most synagogues hold a *Purim Schpeel*, which is a lighthearted performance using modern themes to poke fun at some of the characters in the Purim story.

Purim occurs on the fourteenth day of the Hebrew month of Adar, which usually falls in March.

Passover

Passover, known in Hebrew as *Pesach*, is probably the most widely observed holiday in the Jewish calendar. Occurring in late March or April, it celebrates the Exodus of the Israelites from Egypt as they journeyed from slavery to freedom, from degradation to exaltation. Reform Jews celebrate Pesach for seven days, as do all Jews in Israel. Conservative and Orthodox Jews observe for eight days. Pesach's message is captured in the *seder* ceremony, the extraordinary gathering of family and guests around the dinner table on the first and second nights of the holiday. We use a *haggadah*, an elaborate book which describes the traditions, asks Pesach questions, provides answers, offers songs and sparkling discussion, and provides prominent roles for the children. At the *seder*, family and friends gather to recall and explore the meaning of the Exodus and what it teaches us today about freedom, not only for Jews but for any oppressed people. It carries a powerful message against racism, sexism, and religious persecution, while challenging us to battle against poverty and disease and to work for peace throughout the world. If there are individuals in the community who have no *seder* to attend, it's a *mitzvah* to invite them.

For the duration of Pesach, Jews eat *matzah*, unleavened bread, reminiscent of the dough that baked without rising which the Israelites took with them as they fled Egypt. When we eat matzah, we say:

בָּרוּךְ אַתָּה יְיָ, אֱלֹהֵינוּ מֶלֶךְ הָעוֹלָם, אֲשֶׁר קִדְּשָׁנוּ בְּמִצְוֹתָיו וְצִוָּנוּ עַל אֲכִילַת מַצָּה.

Baruch ata Adonai, Eloheinu melech ha'olam, asher kid'shanu b'mitzvotav v'tzivanu al achilat matzah.

Blessed are You, Adonai our God, Sovereign of the universe, who makes our lives holy through mitzvot and commands us to eat unleavened bread.

Yom HaShoah, Holocaust Memorial Day

In 1951, the Knesset, Israel's parliament, designated 27 Nisan (one week after the seventh day of Pesach) as the day on

which Jews throughout the world would conduct ceremonies to remember the victims of the Shoah (Holocaust). It is a time not only to recall the destruction of European Jewry, but also to commit ourselves to making sure that such a tragedy never happens again.

Most Jewish communities in North America organize programs which include speakers, poetry, and memorial prayers such as *El Male Rachamim* and *kaddish* and lighting *yahrzeit* candles (*yahrzeit* candles traditionally commemorate the year anniversary of a death). Six candles recall the six million Jews who perished in the Holocaust. In our homes, as well, it is appropriate to light a memorial candle. In Israel, at 11:00 a.m. that day, all activity, including traffic, halts for two minutes to pay tribute to the memory of the victims.

Yom Ha'Atzma'ut, Israel Independence Day

The State of Israel was established on the fifth day of Iyar 5708 (May 12, 1948). To express our joy and gratitude for Israel and to emphasize our commitment to its strength and security, Jews throughout the world celebrate the establishment of the Jewish State with Israel Day parades, songs, films, and prayers of thanksgiving. It is appropriate for Reform Jews to make *tzedakah* contributions to Israeli organizations, especially those that are helping to build a pluralistic Jewish society.

Shavuot, the Feast of Weeks

Shavuot is the third of the three pilgrimage festivals known as *chagim*. The other two are Sukkot and Pesach. Shavuot has both an agricultural connection and a religious basis. It celebrates the late spring harvest, coming "a week of weeks" or 49 days after Pesach. Jews traditionally count the 49 days of the *omer*, a measure of barley, from the second night of Pesach until the day before Shavuot. This "counting" serves to connect the festivals of Pesach and Shavuot, thus reminding us that human freedom (as in Pesach) can only endure if it leads to observance of God's commandments (as in Shavuot).

Shavuot also commemorates the time when the Israelites received the Law at Sinai. In the synagogue the Ten Commandments and the Biblical Book of Ruth are chanted. Most synagogues conduct an evening program known as *Tikun Lail Shavuot*, a time when Jews gather, sometimes late into the night, to study and discuss Jewish texts. Confirmation is also held on or near Shavuot. Traditional dairy dishes such as blintzes are eaten. Many reasons are offered for eating dairy, one of which is that by excluding meat, we exercise restraint and self-control. Another is that dairy symbolizes the land of Israel, which the Torah describes as "a land flowing with milk and honey."

Lag B'Omer

On the 33rd day of the counting of the *omer*, Lag B'Omer is celebrated. (The Hebrew letters for "*lag*" stand for 33.) This is a day of celebration, marking a break in the period between Pesach and Shavuot which is traditionally viewed as a mournful time when tragic events occurred in Jewish history. According to Jewish tradition, Rabbi Shimon bar

Yochai, who was sentenced to death by the Romans for leading a revolt against them, hid in a cave, and did not emerge until Lag B'Omer when he was told that his oppressors had been defeated. Jewish schools often celebrate Lag B'Omer with sporting events (as in a Maccabiah), Israeli dancing, picnics, and bonfires. Traditional Jews, who abstain from weddings between *Pesach* and *Shavuot*, may schedule them on *Lag B'Omer*. The holiday is also known as the Scholars Festival. Reform Jews permit weddings during this period.

Tisha b'Av, the Ninth Day of Av

According to tradition, the first Temple in Jerusalem was destroyed by the Babylonians on the ninth day of the Hebrew month of Av, 586 BCE, as was the second Temple by the Romans in the year 70 CE. (BCE stands for "before the Common Era" and CE for "common era".) Other tragic events in Israel's history are also attributed to the ninth of Av. In commemoration, traditional Jews observe a full day of fasting. In many synagogues and Jewish summer camps (the month of Av occurs in mid-summer), a program may include chanting from the Biblical Book of Lamentations and study of a Jewish text.

CHAPTER 8

Life Cycle

*O*NE of the things many people love about being Jewish is the beautiful traditions which we celebrate along every step of the cycle of life. These traditions increase the joy we experience at happy times and strengthen us during difficult times. They also help us better understand the meaning of our lives and distinguish between what is important and what is less important.

At happy occasions, it is appropriate to chant or say the *shehecheyanu* prayer, such as when a child is born or named, at a *B'rit Milah* or circumcision ceremony, at a Bar or Bat Mitzvah, wedding, conversion to Judaism, or celebration of some other significant achievement.

בָּרוּךְ אַתָּה יְיָ אֱלֹהֵינוּ מֶלֶךְ הָעוֹלָם, שֶׁהֶחֱיָנוּ וְקִיְּמָנוּ וְהִגִּיעָנוּ לַזְּמַן הַזֶּה.

Baruch ata Adonai, Eloheinu melech ha'olam, shehecheyanu v'kiy'manu v'higi'anu laz'man hazeh.

Blessed are You, Adonai our God, Sovereign of the

51

universe, who has kept us alive, sustained us, and enabled us to reach this joyous time.

Birth

The birth of a child is an event of enormous significance, not only for the parents and family, but for the synagogue and the Jewish people. The ceremony of circumcision or the naming ceremony offers a blessing for the new baby that looks forward to a life of Torah, *Chuppah*, and *Ma'asim Tovim*.

Torah in its broadest sense means Jewish learning and a fine secular education as well. Jews emphasize education and personal growth as they anticipate the future of a newborn child

Chuppah, literally the wedding canopy, refers to the hope that the infant will grow up to establish his or her own family and a home filled with Jewish traditions and values to inspire and enrich the spirit.

Ma'asim Tovim are "good deeds." We expect that the child will grow up committed to *tikkun olam*, improving the world through acts of kindness, justice, and peace. On behalf of the child, the parents usually make a *tzedakah* contribution to a worthy charity. This gift becomes symbolically the child's first act of philanthropy.

B'rit Milah, Covenant of Circumcision

The act of circumcising male babies on the eighth day is commanded to Abraham in Genesis 17:12. One of the most important rituals in all of Jewish life, it is known as *B'rit*

Milah, the covenant of circumcision, and it connects us to Jews everywhere and to generations of Jews who came before us. The Ashkenazic pronunciation is "*b'ris*," while the Sephardic is "*b'rit*."

In calculating eight days, the day of birth counts as day one. If the boy is born on a Monday, the *B'rit Milah* takes place on the following Monday. Even if the eighth day falls on Shabbat, the *B'rit Milah* occurs on that day, so important is the tradition of the eighth day! (If the baby is weak or ill, however, circumcision may be delayed.)

The *B'rit Milah* is traditionally conducted by a *mohel*, who is expertly trained, both medically and ritually, in circumcision. Reform Judaism has trained dozens of Jewish physicians (men and women) to be expert *mohalim*. A list of Reform-trained *mohalim* is available from the Union for Reform Judaism. (Go to www.urj.org/resources and click "Conversion/Interfaith" and then on "Find A Mohel/et.") It is appropriate to invite your rabbi to participate in the ritual aspect of the *B'rit Milah*.

The arrival of a girl baby is celebrated with *B'rit HaBat*, a covenantal naming ceremony. It is traditional for the ceremony to take place in the synagogue on Shabbat morning as soon as possible after the birth. It may also occur Friday evening or in the home. When the ceremony is held in the synagogue, the parents bring the baby and are joined by family and friends. Such a ceremony may also be held for a boy.

Beginning a Child's Jewish Education

A child's Jewish education should begin as early as possible. For a detailed discussion of Jewish education, see Chapter 5.

Marriage

"It is not good for man to be alone" (Genesis 2:18). Built into the story of creation in Genesis is the centrality of the relationship between man and woman. In the Midrash, the story is told of a Roman matron who asks, "What has God been doing since creation?" The rabbis answer, "Making matches between husbands and wives." The matron responds, "Is that all that your God does? Why, I could do that myself." She then arbitrarily pairs up her male and female slaves. The next morning they show up. One has a broken arm; the other is bruised head to toe; another can barely walk. "Aha," says the matron, "now I see that it is an awesome task to bring a man and woman together in marriage. Your God is indeed great!"

Before officiating at a wedding ceremony, the rabbi will invite the couple to a number of in depth sessions to discuss the ritual and the meaning of marriage and family in Jewish tradition. The rabbi will usually suggest readings for the couple prior to marriage and, where appropriate, may propose some form of premarital counseling or marriage enrichment program.

Just before the ceremony, bride and groom sign a *ketubbah*, or marriage contract, in the presence of witnesses and family. Most Reform couples use a contemporary

ketubbah which describes the spiritual and emotional relationship to which they aspire, a relationship based on the
highest Jewish values.

The Jewish wedding ceremony used to consist of two
parts, now united into one. The first was known as *eirusin*,
the formal betrothal ceremony. The central aspect of *eirusin*
is *kiddushin*, which comes from the Hebrew word *kadosh*,
meaning "holiness." *Kiddushin* is the exchange of rings and
vows between husband and wife ("Be sanctified to me with
this ring as my wife/husband according to the law of Moses
and Israel").

The second part, *nissuin*, brought the bride and groom
under the *chuppah* and marked the formal part of the ceremony, in which the couple is legally married.

The *Sheva B'rachot*, the seven traditional marriage blessings, are recited during this part of the ceremony.

1. בָּרוּךְ אַתָּה יְיָ אֱלֹהֵינוּ מֶלֶךְ הָעוֹלָם, בּוֹרֵא פְּרִי
הַגָּפֶן.

2. בָּרוּךְ אַתָּה יְיָ אֱלֹהֵינוּ מֶלֶךְ הָעוֹלָם, שֶׁהַכֹּל בָּרָא
לִכְבוֹדוֹ.

3. בָּרוּךְ אַתָּה יְיָ אֱלֹהֵינוּ מֶלֶךְ הָעוֹלָם, יוֹצֵר הָאָדָם.

4. בָּרוּךְ אַתָּה יְיָ אֱלֹהֵינוּ מֶלֶךְ הָעוֹלָם, אֲשֶׁר יָצַר אֶת
הָאָדָם בְּצַלְמוֹ, בְּצֶלֶם דְּמוּת תַּבְנִיתוֹ, וְהִתְקִין לוֹ
מִמֶּנּוּ בִּנְיַן עֲדֵי עַד. בָּרוּךְ אַתָּה יְיָ, יוֹצֵר הָאָדָם.

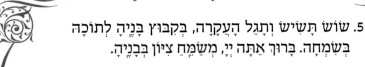

5. שׂוֹשׂ תָּשִׂישׂ וְתָגֵל הָעֲקָרָה, בְּקִבּוּץ בָּנֶיהָ לְתוֹכָהּ בְּשִׂמְחָה. בָּרוּךְ אַתָּה יְיָ, מְשַׂמֵּחַ צִיּוֹן בְּבָנֶיהָ.

6. שַׂמֵּחַ תְּשַׂמַּח רֵעִים הָאֲהוּבִים, כְּשַׂמֵּחֲךָ יְצִירְךָ בְּגַן עֵדֶן מִקֶּדֶם. בָּרוּךְ אַתָּה יְיָ, מְשַׂמֵּחַ חָתָן וְכַלָּה.

7. בָּרוּךְ אַתָּה יְיָ אֱלֹהֵינוּ מֶלֶךְ הָעוֹלָם, אֲשֶׁר בָּרָא שָׂשׂוֹן וְשִׂמְחָה, חָתָן וְכַלָּה, גִּילָה, רִנָּה, דִּיצָה וְחֶדְוָה, אַהֲבָה וְאַחֲוָה וְשָׁלוֹם וְרֵעוּת. מְהֵרָה, יְיָ אֱלֹהֵינוּ, יִשָּׁמַע בְּעָרֵי יְהוּדָה וּבְחֻצוֹת יְרוּשָׁלַיִם, קוֹל שָׂשׂוֹן וְקוֹל שִׂמְחָה, קוֹל חָתָן וְקוֹל כַּלָּה, קוֹל מִצְהֲלוֹת חֲתָנִים מֵחֻפָּתָם וּנְעָרִים מִמִּשְׁתֵּה נְגִינָתָם. בָּרוּךְ אַתָּה יְיָ, מְשַׂמֵּחַ חָתָן עִם הַכַּלָּה.

1. *Baruch ata Adonai, Eloheinu melech ha'olam, borei p'ri hagafen.*

2. *Baruch ata Adonai, Eloheinu melech ha'olam, shehakol bara lichvodo.*

3. *Baruch ata Adonai, Eloheinu melech ha'olam, yotzeir ha'adam.*

4. *Baruch ata Adonai, Eloheinu melech ha'olam asher yatzar et ha'adam b'tzalmo, b'tzelem d'mut tavnito, v'hitkin lo mimenu binyan adei ad. Baruch ata Adonai, yotzeir ha'adam.*

5. *Sos tasis v'tageil Tziyon b'kibbutz baneha l'tochah b'simchah. Baruch ata Adonai, m'sameiach Tziyon b'vaneha.*

6. *Sameiach t'samach rei'im ha'ahuvim k'samei-chacha y'tzircha b'gan eiden mikedem. Baruch ata Adonai, m'sameiach chatan v'challah.*

7. *Baruch ata Adonai, Eloheinu melech ha'olam, asher bara sason v'simchah, chatan v'kallah, gilah, rinah, ditzah v'chedvah, ahavah v'achava, shalom v'reiut. M'heirah, Adonai Eloheinu, yishama b'arei Y'hudah uv'chutzot Y'rushalayim, kol chatan v'kol kallah, kol mitzhalot chatanim meihupatam un'arim mimishtei n'ginatam. Baruch ata Adonai, m'sameiach chatan im hakallah.*

1. We praise You, Adonai our God, Sovereign of the universe, Creator of the fruit of the vine.

2. We praise You, Sovereign of the universe, Creator of all things for Your glory.

3. We praise You, Adonai our God, Sovereign of the universe, Creator of man and woman.

4. We praise You, Adonai our God, Sovereign of the universe, who creates us as partners with You in life's everlasting renewal.

5. We praise You, Adonai our God, Sovereign of the universe, who causes Zion to rejoice in her children's happy return.

6. We praise You, Adonai our God, Sovereign of the universe, who causes bride and groom to rejoice. May these loving companions rejoice as have Your creatures since the days of creation.

7. We praise You, Adonai our God, Sovereign of the universe, Creator of joy and gladness, bride and groom, love and kinship, peace, and friendship. O God, may there always be heard in the cities of Israel and in the streets of Jerusalem: the sounds of joy and of happiness, the voice of the groom and the voice of the bride, the shouts of young people celebrating, the

songs of children at play. We praise You, our God, who causes bride and groom to rejoice together.

(*Rabbi's Manual*, Central Conference of American Rabbis, pp. 62–64)

During the ceremony, the rabbi addresses the bride and groom, sharing personal reflections based on his or her experiences and conversations with the couple and on insights from Jewish tradition

The ceremony concludes with a blessing by the rabbi and the breaking of the glass. There are many explanations for the breaking of the glass. One is that it recalls the destruction of the ancient Temple in Jerusalem in 70 CE. It reminds us that even in the midst of great personal joy, we are part of the ongoing process of Jewish history, a history that is enriched by this *chuppah*.

Following the ceremony, the couple enjoys some moments of privacy. Known as *yichud*, this interval affords bride and groom an opportunity to be alone and to share the spirit of the occasion before greeting guests at the reception.

It is traditional to conclude the reception celebration with *Birkat Hamazon* (See Chapter 6) followed by another recitation of the *Sheva B'rachot*, with the blessing for wine at the end.

In 2000, Reform rabbis, meeting at the Central Conference of American Rabbis, voted unanimously that "the relationship of Jewish same-gender couples is worthy of affirmation through Jewish ritual." Many Reform rabbis today officiate at same-gender unions because they believe

that such ceremonies of commitment deserve to be sancti-fied by Jewish ritual.

Establishing a Jewish Home

When establishing a Jewish home, it is important to find a town, city, or neighborhood that has a synagogue and a Jewish community. When you move into an apartment or house, one of the first things to do is affix a *mezuzah* on the doorpost of the entrance and, if you wish, at the entrance to each room. The *mezuzah* is a small case with parchment inside containing the *Sh'ma* and an accompanying passage from Deuteronomy 6:4–9. If you move, you should detach the *mezuzah* and take it with you.

This is the blessing for affixing the *mezuzah:*

בָּרוּךְ אַתָּה יְיָ אֱלֹהֵינוּ מֶלֶךְ הָעוֹלָם, אֲשֶׁר קִדְּשָׁנוּ
בְּמִצְוֹתָיו, וְצִוָּנוּ לִקְבֹּעַ מְזוּזָה.

Baruch ata Adonai, Eloheinu melech ha'olam, asher kid'shanu b'mitzvotav v'tzivanu likboa mezuzah.

Blessed are You, Adonai, our God, Sovereign of the universe, who makes our lives holy through mitzvot and commands us to affix the *mezuzah.*

This is followed by the *Shehecheyanu* prayer.

Jewish books, magazines, CDs, ritual objects (such as *Kiddush* cups and Shabbat candlesticks), and artwork enhance the Jewish character of our homes.

Wedding Anniversary

On the anniversary of a wedding (especially a major one, such as 18, 25, 36, 50, or 60), it is inspiring to attend Shabbat services (evening or morning) and, when appropriate, to be called to the Torah for an *aliyah* and to be blessed by the rabbi. Family and friends are usually invited to share this *simcha*.

Death

When a loved one dies, we need all the help we can muster to deal with our sadness, prepare for the days and weeks ahead, and eventually summon the strength to return to the tasks of life. Jewish tradition – based on the wisdom of the ages – is exceedingly helpful at this time. Your rabbi who is uniquely trained to guide you through this process should be contacted immediately. He or she can also provide you with books and pamphlets that offer guidance and insight.

On being informed of a death, it is appropriate to say the following:

בָּרוּךְ אַתָּה יְיָ, דַּיַּן הָאֱמֶת.

Baruch ata Adonai, Dayan ha'emet.
Blessed are You, Adonai, Judge of truth.

The funeral should be held as soon as possible. It consists of prayers and psalms, a *hesped* or eulogy by the rabbi, and the *El Male Rachamim* prayer. The Mourner's *Kaddish* is pronounced at the cemetery.

MOURNER'S KADDISH

The Mourner's Kaddish is one of the most powerful and helpful prayers in all of Jewish tradition. In the words of our prayer book, "The Kaddish possesses wonderful power. It keeps the living together and forms a bridge to the mysterious realm of the dead. Can a people disappear and be annihilated so long as a child remembers its parents?"

(Adapted from *Gates of Prayer*, Central Conference of American Rabbis, New York N.Y. p. 622)

The Mourner's Kaddish makes no mention of death but is rather a praise of God and an affirmation of life. It is appropriate to say the Mourner's Kaddish at the time of burial at the cemetery, during *shiva* (see the next section), throughout the year of mourning, at *yahrzeit* (anniversary of the day of death), and during *Yizkor* memorial services.

יִתְגַּדַּל וְיִתְקַדַּשׁ שְׁמֵהּ רַבָּא. בְּעָלְמָא דִּי בְרָא כִרְעוּתֵהּ, וְיַמְלִיךְ מַלְכוּתֵהּ בְּחַיֵּיכוֹן וּבְיוֹמֵיכוֹן וּבְחַיֵּי דְכָל בֵּית יִשְׂרָאֵל, בַּעֲגָלָא וּבִזְמַן קָרִיב, וְאִמְרוּ אָמֵן.

יְהֵא שְׁמֵהּ רַבָּא מְבָרַךְ לְעָלַם וּלְעָלְמֵי עָלְמַיָּא.

יִתְבָּרַךְ וְיִשְׁתַּבַּח וְיִתְפָּאַר וְיִתְרוֹמַם וְיִתְנַשֵּׂא וְיִתְהַדָּר וְיִתְעַלֶּה וְיִתְהַלָּל שְׁמֵהּ דְּקֻדְשָׁא בְּרִיךְ הוּא, לְעֵלָּא מִן כָּל בִּרְכָתָא וְשִׁירָתָא תֻּשְׁבְּחָתָא וְנֶחֱמָתָא, דַּאֲמִירָן בְּעָלְמָא, וְאִמְרוּ אָמֵן.

יְהֵא שְׁלָמָא רַבָּא מִן שְׁמַיָּא, וְחַיִּים עָלֵינוּ וְעַל כָּל יִשְׂרָאֵל, וְאִמְרוּ אָמֵן.

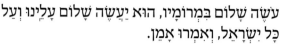

עֹשֶׂה שָׁלוֹם בִּמְרוֹמָיו, הוּא יַעֲשֶׂה שָׁלוֹם עָלֵינוּ וְעַל
כָּל יִשְׂרָאֵל, וְאִמְרוּ אָמֵן.

Yitgadal v'yitkadash sh'mei rabba, b'alma div'ra chir'utei,
v'yamlich malchutei b'cha-yeichon uv'yomeichon uv'chay-
yei d'chol beit Yisrael, ba'agala uvizman kariv, v'imru:
amein

Y'hei sh'mei rabba m'vorach l'alam ul'almei almaya.

Yitbarach v'yishtabach v'yitpa'ar v'yitromam v'yitnasei,
v'yithadar v'yit'aleh v'yithalal sh'mei d'kud'sha, b'rich hu,
l'eila min kol birchata v'shirata, tushb'chata v'nechemata
da'amiran b'alma v'imru: amein.

Y'hei sh'lama rabba min-sh'maya v'chayyim aleinu v'al kol
Yisrael v'imru: amein.

Oseh shalom bim'romav hu ya'aseh shalom aleinu v'al kol
Yisrael v'imru: amein.

Let the glory of God be extolled, and God's great
name be hallowed in the world whose creation God
willed. May God rule in our own day, in our own lives,
and in the life of all Israel, and let us say: Amen.

Let God's great name be blessed for ever and ever.

Beyond all the praises, songs, and adorations that we
can utter is the Holy One, the Blessed One, whom yet
we glorify, honor, and exalt. And let us say: Amen.

For us and for all Israel, may the blessing of peace and
the promise of life come true, and let us say: Amen.

May God who makes peace in the high places, bring
peace to us and to all Israel, and let us say: Amen.

(Translation adapted from *Gates of Prayer for*
Shabbat and Weekdays, Central Conference of
American Rabbis).

At the conclusion of the interment at the cemetery, mourners will place earth on the casket, a final act of respect for the deceased.

When the bereaved family returns home after a funeral, the family lights the memorial candle and says the following:

נֵר יי נִשְׁמַת אָדָם. בָּרוּךְ אַתָּה יי, נֹטֵעַ בְּתוֹכֵנוּ חַיֵּי עוֹלָם.

Ner Adonai nishmat adam. Baruch ata Adonai, notei'a b'tocheinu chayei olam.

The human spirit is the lamp of Adonai. Praised is Adonai, who has implanted within us eternal life.

After lighting the candle, the family gathers about the table and joins in *Motzee*, the blessing over bread. Sharing bread together is an initial step in returning to the tasks of life.

SHIVA, THE SEVEN DAYS OF MOURNING

Shiva is the period of mourning which lasts for seven days. (*Shiva* literally means "seven.") In counting the days of *shiva*, keep in mind that a day in the Jewish calendar begins and ends at sunset. Part of a day counts as a full day. Mourners do not sit *shiva* on Shabbat. After those calculations, the number of days on which mourners formally sit *shiva* is closer to five. In certain circumstances, mourners may elect to observe three days.

When offering comfort to mourners, either through a written note or when visiting, it is appropriate to say:

הַמָּקוֹם יְנַחֵם אֶתְכֶם בְּתוֹךְ אֲבֵלֵי צִיּוֹן וִירוּשָׁלָיִם

HaMakom yinachem etchem b'toch avlei Tziyon v'Yerushalayim.

May God comfort you amidst the mourners for Zion and Jerusalem.

CHAPTER 9

The State of Israel, *Medinat Yisrael*

*T*HE State of Israel is the homeland of the Jewish people. It was there that the patriarchs and matriarchs of Judaism built up our people. It was there that the kings of Judah and Israel reigned, where prophets preached the word of God, where the Temple in Jerusalem was erected, where synagogues were established, where academies of learning flourished, and where great centers of commerce prospered.

After a long period of exile, Jews in the late nineteenth and early twentieth centuries undertook a renewed effort to resettle the land. On May 14, 1948, the modern state of Israel was established by 600,000 pioneers and was immediately recognized as a sovereign nation by the United States and other nations. On May 11, 1949, Israel was accepted into membership in the United Nations. It is a privilege to be alive at this momentous time in human history, when we can experience the dramatic rebirth of the Jewish State, the renewal of Jewish culture, and the security that comes with Jewish political independence

Today the population of Israel numbers six million, of whom 20 percent are non-Jews. The Law of Return guarantees any Jew in the world the right of citizenship – an assured haven from persecution. Had Israel existed in the late 1930s, many Jews would have survived Hitler's madness by emigrating to the Jewish State.

In Israel, the Hebrew language has come alive and Jewish culture thrives. This fact has infused Jewish life in North America and throughout the world with a new dynamism and sense of confidence. Israel's museums, universities, theater, music, and dance are world class; her archaeological sites are second to none. Research in technology and medicine have improved the lives of people all over the world, especially in third-world countries afflicted by poverty and disease. Israel's major cities – Jerusalem, Tel Aviv, Haifa, and Eilat – offer tourist accommodations, restaurants, beaches, and culture of the highest order. It is a mitzvah to visit Israel, where sojourns in her smaller cities, kibbutzim, villages, and countryside enable us to experience the beauty of nature and the drama of our history.

Shabbat in Israel can be a powerful spiritual experience, as work ceases, synagogues are filled with worshippers, and a sense of *shalom*, of peace, abounds. Progressive synagogues affiliated with the Reform movement are available throughout the country, including Congregation Kol HaNeshama in Jerusalem, Or Chadash in Haifa, and Bet Daniel in north

Tel Aviv. Smaller towns and suburbs also offer outstanding Progressive synagogues.

The Hebrew Union College–Jewish Institute of Religion, our Reform seminary, proudly maintains an extraordinary campus on King David Street in Jerusalem where rabbinic, cantorial, and education students from its US campus study for a year, Many Israeli students also prepare for the rabbinate at the Jerusalem campus.

Reform Jews in North America support the Israel Movement for Progressive Judaism (IMPJ), which offers a much needed pluralistic, egalitarian interpretation of Judaism. The IMPJ is building a network of liberal synagogues, schools, and settlements as well as the Religious Action Center in Jerusalem. The Israel Movement's mission is to provide Israelis with an alternative to a rigid, unyielding approach to Judaism and to ensure equal rights for Reform and Conservative Jews in Israel, including our rabbis and our institutions. The Israeli rabbis ordained by Hebrew Union College in Jerusalem are providing the leadership to respond to these challenges.

Among the outstanding opportunities for North American youth to visit Israel are the summer and year-long programs of the North American Federation of Temple Youth (NFTY, an arm of the Union for Reform Judaism), Birthright Israel (for college students), and trips from individual synagogues and Jewish federations. "Going up to Jerusalem" is known as "making *aliyah*." *Aliyah* is the same word that we use for being called to the Torah for a blessing and for settling in Israel.

The World Union for Progressive Judaism (WUPJ) provides indispensible financial and staff support for Progressive Judaism in Israel and throughout the world. The World Union plays a significant role in implementing a vision for a pluralistic Jewish life in Israel. It also actively encourages Progressive Judaism in Russia, Ukraine and other countries of the former Soviet Union, as well as Europe, Asia and other continents.

ARZA, the Association of Reform Zionists of America (and its counterpart ARZA Canada) are the Zionist arms of the Reform Movement in North America. Their mission is to educate Reform Jews about Israel, emphasize the centrality of Israel in Jewish life, encourage programs which support the Jewish State and sponsor travel to Israel. By becoming members of ARZA, individual Reform Jews help to strengthen ARZA's important work on behalf of Israel.

On Traveling to Israel

The following prayer may be said on arrival in Israel:

As we set foot (once more) in this old-new land – steeped in sacred memories, great achievements and noble hopes – deep feelings of belonging are stirred within us. We recite the words of the ancient pilgrim as if they had been written for us:

(Adapted from *Siddur Lev Chadash*, Union of Liberal and Progressive Synagogues, London)

שָׂמַחְתִּי בְּאֹמְרִים לִי, בֵּית יי נֵלֵךְ

Samachti b'omrim li, beit Adonai neileich.

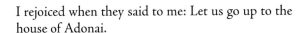

I rejoiced when they said to me: Let us go up to the house of Adonai.

עוֹמְדוֹת הָיוּ רַגְלֵינוּ בִּשְׁעָרַיִךְ, יְרוּשָׁלַיִם

Omdot hayu ragleinu bisharayich, Yerushalayim.

Now we are standing within your gates, O Jerusalem!

יְבָרֶכֵנִי יי מִצִיּוֹן. שָׁלוֹם עַל יִשְׂרָאֵל.

Yivar'cheini Adonai miTziyon. Shalom al Yisrael.

May Adonai bless us from Zion.

May there be peace upon Israel.

CHAPTER 10

Texts for Study: Moral and Ethical Teachings from Jewish Tradition

The Ten Commandments

1. I am Adonai, your God, who brought you out of the land of Egypt, out of the house of bondage. You shall have no other gods besides Me.
2. You shall not make for yourself a carved image or any figure that is in the heavens above, that is on the earth beneath, or that is in the waters beneath the earth. You shall not bow down to them nor serve them.
3. You shall not swear falsely by the name of Adonai, your God.
4. Remember the Sabbath day and keep it holy.
5. Honor your father and your mother.
6. You shall not murder.
7. You shall not commit adultery.
8. You shall not steal.

9. You shall not testify against another person as a false witness.
10. You shall not covet.

– Exodus 20

You shall be holy, for I, Adonai, your God, am holy.
– Leviticus 19

Do not separate yourself from the community;
Do not be certain of yourself until the day you die;
Do not judge others until you are in their place;
And do not say : "When I have leisure I shall study."
You may never have leisure.

– Rabbi Akiva

If I am not for myself, who will be for me?
But if I am for myself alone, what am I?
And if not now, when?

– Rabbi Hillel

You are not required to complete the task,
But neither are you free to abstain from it altogether.
– Rabbi Tarfon

When two persons sit anad words of Torah pass between them, The Divine Presence dwells in their midst.

– Rabbi Chananyah ben Teradyon

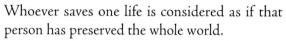

Whoever saves one life is considered as if that person has preserved the whole world.

– The Talmud

Prosperity obtained through truth and righteousness is built on a sure rock.
Happiness derived from falsehood, injustice, and lust is built on sand.

– Maimonides

Why I Am a Jew

I am a Jew because, born of Israel and having lost her, I have felt her live again in me, more loving than myself.

I am a Jew because, born of Israel and having regained her, I wish her to live after me, more living than myself.

I am a Jew because the faith of Israel demands of me no abdication of the mind.

I am a Jew because the faith of Israel requires of me all the devotion of my heart.

I am a Jew because in every place where suffering weeps, the Jew weeps.

I am a Jew because every time despair cries out, the Jew hopes.

I am a Jew because the promise of Israel is the universal promise.

I am a Jew because, for Israel, the world is not yet completed; we are completing it.

I am a Jew because for Israel, humanity is not yet fully formed; humanity must perfect itself.

– Edmund Fleg

So many people go through life filling the store-room of their minds with odds and ends of a grudge here, a jealousy there, a pettiness, a selfishness – all ignoble. The true task of a man is to create a noble memory, a mind filled with grandeur, forgiveness, restless ideals, and the dynamic ethical ferment preached by all religions at their best.

– Rabbi Leo Baeck

CHAPTER II

Private Prayers, Songs, and Psalms

Private Prayers

ON GOING TO SLEEP AT NIGHT

Thank You, Eternal God, for the day that is now ending; for the blessings it has brought to me and those I love, and for any good that I may have done.

At this late hour, grant me tranquility of spirit, that I may have a restful night and rise in the morning with renewed strength for Your service.

(*Siddur Lev Chadash*, Union of Liberal and Progresive Synagogues, London)

בְּיָדוֹ אַפְקִיד רוּחִי, בְּעֵת אִישַׁן וְאָעִירָה. וְעִם רוּחִי גְּוִיָּתִי, יְיָ לִי וְלֹא אִירָא.

B'yado afkid ruchi, B'eit ishan v'a-ira. V'im ruchi g'viyati, Adonai li, v'lo i-ra.

Into your hands I give my soul, Both when I sleep and when I wake; And with my soul, my body too. Adonai is with me, I do not fear.

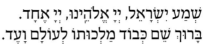

שְׁמַע יִשְׂרָאֵל, יְיָ אֱלֹהֵינוּ, יְיָ אֶחָד.
בָּרוּךְ שֵׁם כְּבוֹד מַלְכוּתוֹ לְעוֹלָם וָעֶד.

Sh'ma Yisrael Adonai Eloheinu, Adonai echad.
Baruch sheim k'vod malchuto l'olam va'ed.

Listen, O Israel: Adonai is our God, Adonai is One.
Praised is God's glorious majesty forever and ever.

ON RISING UP IN THE MORNING

Thank You, Eternal God, for the gift of this new day, and help me to use it well. Keep me mindful of my responsibilities as a human being, created in Your image, and as a member of the House of Israel. Make me strong against temptation, discouragement, and adversity. Let me not hurt others, but rather contribute to their happiness and well-being. And may I add a little to the sum total of goodness in Your world.

> (*Siddur Lev Chadash*, Union of Liberal and Progresive Synagogues, London)

וְטַהֵר לִבִּי לְעָבְדְּךָ בֶּאֱמֶת

V'taheir libi l'ovd'cha be'emet

O God, purify my heart that I may serve You in truth.

שְׁמַע יִשְׂרָאֵל, יְיָ אֱלֹהֵינוּ, יְיָ אֶחָד.
בָּרוּךְ שֵׁם כְּבוֹד מַלְכוּתוֹ לְעוֹלָם וָעֶד.

Sh'ma Yisrael Adonai Eloheinu, Adonai echad.
Baruch sheim k'vod malchuto l'olam va'ed.

Listen, O Israel: Adonai is our God, Adonai is One.
Praised is God's glorious majesty forever and ever.

WHEN WE BEHOLD THE BEAUTY OF NATURE

A person who can no longer pause to wonder and stand rapt in awe is as good as dead; his eyes are closed. (Albert Einstein)

בָּרוּךְ אַתָּה יְיָ אֱלֹהֵינוּ מֶלֶךְ הָעוֹלָם, עוֹשֶׂה מַעֲשֶׂה בְּרֵאשִׁית.

Baruch ata Adonai, Eloheinu melech ha'olam, oseh ma'aseh b'reshit.

Blessed is Adonai, our God, Sovereign of the universe, who has created the glories of nature.

PRAYERS FOR HEALING

Bikkur cholim, visiting the sick, is an important mitzvah. Our visits bring to an ill person support, strength, and a sense that we truly care. The tradition of offering prayers for the sick at the synagogue, which also supports the healing process, is a frequent practice and is appreciated by the ill person and the family.

WHEN VISITING THE SICK

We are grateful, O God, for the gift of life and for the healing power that You have implanted within Your creatures. Sustain ...., our loved one, through these days of illness with the courage and strength that (he) (she) needs to endure discomfort. May those who minister to .... be endowed with skill and caring. May the difficulty soon be ended and may .... return in health to family and friends.

(Adapted, *Gates of the House*, Central Conference of American Rabbis, p. 159)

בָּרוּךְ אַתָּה יְיָ, רוֹפֵי הַחוֹלִים.

Baruch ata Adonai, rofei hacholim.

Blessed are You, the Source of healing.

MI SHEBEIRACH PRAYER

מִי שֶׁבֵּרַךְ אֲבוֹתֵינוּ מְקוֹר הַבְּרָכָה לְאִמּוֹתֵינוּ

Mi shebeirach avoteinu, M'kor hab'racha l'imoteinu

May the Source of strength who blessed the ones
before us help us find the courage to make our lives
a blessing
and let us say, Amen.

מִי שֶׁבֵּרַךְ אִמּוֹתֵינוּ מְקוֹר הַבְּרָכָה לַאֲבוֹתֵינוּ

Mi shebeirach imoteinu, M'kor hab'racha la'avoteinu

Bless those in need of healing with *refuah sh'leima*,
the renewal of body, the renewal of spirit, and let us
say, Amen.

(Debbie Friedman and Drorah Setel)

FOR RECOVERY FROM ILLNESS OR ESCAPE FROM DANGER

בָּרוּךְ אַתָּה יְיָ אֱלֹהֵינוּ מֶלֶךְ הָעוֹלָם, שֶׁגְּמָלַנִי כָּל
טוֹב.

*Baruch ata Adonai, Eloheinu melech ha'olam, sheg'malani
kol tov.*

Blessed are You, Adonai our God, Sovereign of the
universe, who has brought great goodness upon me.

Songs for Shabbat and Other Times

SHALOM ALEICHEM

שָׁלוֹם עֲלֵיכֶם, מַלְאֲכֵי הַשָּׁרֵת, מַלְאֲכֵי עֶלְיוֹן, מִמֶּלֶךְ
מַלְכֵי הַמְּלָכִים, הַקָּדוֹשׁ בָּרוּךְ הוּא:

Shalom aleichem malachei hashareit, malachei elyon,
Mimelech malachei ham'lachim, hakadosh baruch hu.

בּוֹאֲכֶם לְשָׁלוֹם, מַלְאֲכֵי הַשָּׁלוֹם, מַלְאֲכֵי עֶלְיוֹן,
מִמֶּלֶךְ מַלְכֵי הַמְּלָכִים, הַקָּדוֹשׁ בָּרוּךְ הוּא:

Bo'achem l'shalom, malachei hashalom, malachei elyon,
Mimelech malachei ham'lachim, hakadosh baruch hu.

בָּרְכוּנִי לְשָׁלוֹם, מַלְאֲכֵי הַשָּׁלוֹם, מַלְאֲכֵי עֶלְיוֹן,
מִמֶּלֶךְ מַלְכֵי הַמְּלָכִים, הַקָּדוֹשׁ בָּרוּךְ הוּא:

Bar'chuni l'shalom, malachei hashalom, malachei elyon,
Mimelech malachei ham'lachim, hakadosh baruch hu.

צֵאתְכֶם לְשָׁלוֹם, מַלְאֲכֵי הַשָּׁלוֹם, מַלְאֲכֵי עֶלְיוֹן,
מִמֶּלֶךְ מַלְכֵי הַמְּלָכִים, הַקָּדוֹשׁ בָּרוּךְ הוּא:

Tzeit'chem l'shalom, malachei hashalom, malachei elyon,
Mimelech malachei ham'lachim, hakadosh baruch hu.

L'CHA DODI

לְכָה דוֹדִי לִקְרַאת כַּלָּה, פְּנֵי שַׁבָּת נְקַבְּלָה.

L'cha dodi likrat kallah, p'nei Shabbat n'kabb'lah.

שָׁמוֹר וְזָכוֹר בְּדִבּוּר אֶחָד, הִשְׁמִיעָנוּ אֵל הַמְּיֻחָד, יְיָ
אֶחָד וּשְׁמוֹ אֶחָד, לְשֵׁם וּלְתִפְאֶרֶת וְלִתְהִלָּה.

Shamor v'zachor b'dibur echad, Hishmianu eil ham'yuchad.
Adonai echad ush'mo echad, L'shaim ul'tiferet v'lit'hilah.

לְכָה דוֹדִי לִקְרַאת כַּלָּה, פְּנֵי שַׁבָּת נְקַבְּלָה.

L'cha dodi likrat kallah, p'nei Shabbat n'kabb'lah.

לִקְרַאת שַׁבָּת לְכוּ וְנֵלְכָה, כִּי הִיא מְקוֹר הַבְּרָכָה,
מֵרֹאשׁ מִקֶּדֶם נְסוּכָה, סוֹף מַעֲשֶׂה בְּמַחֲשָׁבָה
תְּחִלָּה.

Likrat shabat l'chu v'neilchah, Ki hi m'kor hab'rachah.
Meirosh mikedem n'suchah, Sof ma'aseh b'machashavah
t'hilah.

לְכָה דוֹדִי לִקְרַאת כַּלָּה, פְּנֵי שַׁבָּת נְקַבְּלָה.

L'cha dodi likrat kallah, p'nei Shabbat n'kabb'lah

הִתְעוֹרְרִי הִתְעוֹרְרִי, כִּי בָא אוֹרֵךְ קוּמִי אוֹרִי, עוֹרִי
עוֹרִי שִׁיר דַּבֵּרִי, כְּבוֹד יְיָ עָלַיִךְ נִגְלָה.

Hitor'ri hitor'ri, Ki va oreich kumi ori. Uri, uri shir dabeiri,
K'vod Adonai alayich niglah.

לְכָה דוֹדִי לִקְרַאת כַּלָּה, פְּנֵי שַׁבָּת נְקַבְּלָה.

L'cha dodi likrat kallah, p'nei Shabbat n'kabb'lah.

בּוֹאִי בְשָׁלוֹם עֲטֶרֶת בַּעְלָהּ, גַּם בְּשִׂמְחָה וּבְצָהֳלָה,
תּוֹךְ אֱמוּנֵי עַם סְגֻלָּה, בּוֹאִי כַלָּה, בּוֹאִי כַלָּה.

Bo'i v'shalom ateret balah, Gam b'simchah uv'tzaholah.
Toch emunei am s'gulah, Bo'i kallah, bo'i kallah.

לְכָה דוֹדִי לִקְרַאת כַּלָּה, פְּנֵי שַׁבָּת נְקַבְּלָה.

L'cha dodi likrat kallah, p'nei Shabbat n'kabb'lah

MAH YAFEH HAYOM

מַה־יָּפֶה הַיּוֹם, שַׁבָּת שָׁלוֹם.

Mah yafeh hayom, Shabbat shalom,
Mah yafeh hayom, Shabbat shalom
Shabbat, Shabbat shalom
Shabbat, Shabbat shalom
Shabbat, Shabbat shalom
Shabbat shalom.

BIM BAM

בִּים בָּם, שַׁבָּת שָׁלוֹם.

Bim bam, bim bim bim bam
Bim bim bim bim, bim bam. } 2×

Shabbat shalom, Shabbat shalom,
Shabbat, Shabbat, Shabbat, Shabbat, shalom. } 2×

HINEI MAH TOV

הִנֵּה מַה־טּוֹב וּמַה־נָּעִים שֶׁבֶת אַחִים גַּם־יָחַד.

Hinei mah tov umanayim
Shevet achim gam yachad.

LO YISA GOY

לֹא יִשָּׂא גוֹי אֶל גּוֹי חֶרֶב וְלֹא יִלְמְדוּ עוֹד מִלְחָמָה.

Lo yisa goy el goy cherev.
Lo yilm'du od milchamah.

DAVID MELECH

דָּוִד מֶלֶךְ יִשְׂרָאֵל חַי וְקַיָּם.

David melech Yisrael,
chai chai v'kayam.

EILEH CHAMDA LIBI

אֵלֶּה חָמְדָה לִבִּי, וְחוּסָה נָא וְאַל תִּתְעַלָּם.

Eileh chamda libi
Chusa na v'al na titaleim.

AL SH'LOSHA D'VARIM

עַל שְׁלֹשָׁה דְבָרִים הָעוֹלָם עוֹמֵד: עַל הַתּוֹרָה וְעַל
הָעֲבוֹדָה וְעַל גְּמִילוּת חֲסָדִים:

Al sh'losha d'varim
Ha'olam omeid
Al haTorah, v'al ha'avodah,
V'al g'milut chasadim.

HATIKVAH, NATIONAL ANTHEM OF THE STATE OF ISRAEL

כָּל־עוֹד בַּלֵּבָב פְּנִימָה
נֶפֶשׁ יְהוּדִי הוֹמִיָּה
וּלְפַאֲתֵי מִזְרָח קָדִימָה
עַיִן לְצִיּוֹן צוֹפִיָּה.

עוֹד לֹא אָבְדָה תִּקְוָתֵנוּ,
הַתִּקְוָה בַּת שְׁנוֹת אַלְפַּיִם,
לִהְיוֹת עַם חָפְשִׁי בְּאַרְצֵנוּ,
אֶרֶץ צִיּוֹן וִירוּשָׁלָיִם.

Kol od baleivav p'nima
Nefesh Yehudi homiyah
Ul'fa'a'tei mizrach kadima
Ayin l'Tziyon tzofiyah.
Od lo avda tikvateinu

Hatikva sh'not alpayim
L'h'yot am chofshi b'artseinu
B'eretz Tziyon virushalayim. } 2×

Psalms for Living

PSALM 23

> Adonai is my shepherd, I shall not want.
> You make me lie down in green pastures.
> You lead me beside still waters.
> You restore my soul.
> You guide me in straight paths for the sake of Your name.
> Even when I walk through the valley of the shadow of death,
> I will fear no evil, for You are with me.
> Your rod and staff, they comfort me.
> You prepare a table before me in the presence of my enemies.
> You have anointed my head with oil; my cup overflows.
> Surely goodness and mercy shall follow me all the days of my life,
> And I shall dwell in the house of God forever.

PSALM 24 (1–6)

> The earth belongs to Adonai, and all that is within it, the world and they who dwell within.
> For God founded it upon the seas and established it upon the streams.

Who shall ascend the mountain of Adonai?
Who may stand in God's holy place?
Whoever has clean hands and a pure heart,
Who has not taken God's name in vain
And has not sworn deceitfully.
Such a person will receive a blessing from Adonai,
And righteousness from the God of salvation.
Such is the generation who turn to God,
Who seek Your presence, O Jacob.

PSALM 121

I lift my eyes to the mountains;
What is the source of my help?
My help comes from Adonai,
Maker of heaven and earth.
God will not let your foot give way;
Your Protector will not slumber.
See, the Protector of Israel neither slumbers nor
sleeps!
Adonai is your Guardian,
Adonai is your protection at your right hand.
The sun will not strike you by day,
Nor the moon by night.
Adonai will guard you from all harm.
Adonai will guard your soul.
Adonai will guard your going and coming.
Now and forever.

PSALM 130

Out of the depths, I cry to You, Adonai.

Hear my voice, Adonai,
Be attentive to my plea for mercy.
If you keep account of sins
Adonai, who can stand before you?
Yours is the power to forgive,
That You may be held in awe.
I wait for Adonai.
My soul awaits God's words.
I am more eager for God
Even than the watchmen for the morning.
Let Israel wait for Adonai.
For with Adonai is consistent love
and much power to redeem
God will deliver Israel from all its iniquities.

CHAPTER 12

Organizations and Institutions of Reform Judaism

Central Conference of American Rabbis (CCAR)
www.ccarnet.org

Hebrew Union College-Jewish Institute of Religion
(HUC-JIR) www.huc.edu

Union for Reform Judaism (URJ) www.urj.org

Links to the following affiliates of the Union for Reform
Judaism may be found at www.urj.org/dir

American Conference of Cantors (ACC)
Association of Reform Zionists of America (ARZA)
ARZA Canada
Berit Milah Board of Reform Judaism
Early Childhood Educators of Reform Judaism (ECERJ)
Israel Movement for Progressive Judaism (IMPJ)
Israel Religious Action Center (IRAC)

National Association of Temple Educators (NATE)
National Association of Temple Administrators (NATA)
North American Federation of Temple Brotherhoods (NFTB)
North American Federation of Jewish Youth (NFTY)
Program Directors of Reform Judaism (PDRJ)
Progressive Association of Reform Day Schools (PARDES)
Religious Action Center (RAC)
Women of Reform Judaism (WRJ)
World Union for Progressive Judaism (WUPJ)